# FROM SEMINARIAN TO DIOCESAN PRIEST

## Managing a Successful Transition

J. Ronald Knott

Sophronismos Press
Louisville, Kentucky

# FROM SEMINARIAN TO DIOCESAN PRIEST
## Managing a Successful Transition

First Printing: October 2004
ISBN 0-9668969-5-5

*To our future priests,
especially those young men
who are responding courageously
to the call to diocesan priesthood
in today's church.*

# Also by J. Ronald Knott

**For information about where to purchase eBook and
printed editions of Father Knott's books,
go to: www.ronknottbooks.com**

# ACKNOWLEDGMENTS

I would especially like to thank the priests who taught me at Saint Thomas Seminary (1958-1964), the monks of Saint Meinrad Seminary (1964-1970) and the priests of the Louisville Presbyterate who have mentored me since my ordination in 1970. I would like to thank in a very special way Archbishop Thomas C. Kelly, O.P., my bishop, who has always given me the freedom to explore new ministry possibilities as a priest.

I would like to thank those who read this manuscript and offered valuable constructive criticism and encouragement: David Gaffney (a special seminary student from the Nashville diocese), Linda Banker (Associate Vocation Director of the Archdiocese of Louisville), Sister Shirley Ann Warner, O.S.U. (Director of Supervised Ministry and instructor in pastoral studies) and Father Bernard Lutz (Pastor in Residence at Saint Meinrad School of Theology).

Last, but certainly not least, I thank Lori Massey for editing and formatting the manuscript into a book and Tim Schoenbachler for preparing this new edition.

*It is one thing to pledge one's life to a high purpose, but it is another thing to carry through on that pledge.*

*from the Introduction*

# Table of Contents

# INTRODUCTION

*Courage is being scared to death, but saddling up anyway.*
John Wayne

A seminary, in its root meaning, is a place where seeds are germinated and plants are propagated for transplantation – a greenhouse, if you will. By its very nature, a seminary is a temporary, protected, controlled and intensely monitored environment where budding plants are nurtured until they are mature enough to survive transplantation and thrive in a normal growing environment. The transition from protected environment to normal environment requires careful attention. If the plants are immature or the environment is harsh, this transition may cause the plants to go into shock. When in shock, plants often quit growing and become susceptible to disease. All plants experience some degree of shock when they undergo transplantation, but when the shock is too great, they often die.

A seminary is also a place where young men are trained in preparation for transplantation into ministry positions in the Church as priests. For most diocesan priests that means service in parish ministry. By its very nature a seminary is a temporary, protected, controlled and intensely monitored environment. It is a world set apart from the normal environment where discipleship is lived out in the Church and in the world. Like plants, the transplantation from seminary to parish can cause those making the transition to experience their own version of shock, making them susceptible to a host of problems that could lead to leaving ministry altogether.

While the Church has always lost a few priests after ordination, it is becoming a serious problem today. Our current practice of ordaining new priests and then sending them into shrinking and demoralized presbyterates to fend for themselves is showing itself to be a very dangerous practice indeed. With 10%-15% of the newly ordained today not making it past their first five years of priesthood and many more struggling to keep going, the facts seem to be telling us that not enough attention is being paid to the transition from seminary into ministry.

While thirty-five years of priesthood do not necessarily make me an expert, I do have some experience to share. I have survived my own shaky transition from seminary into ministry. I have served as a diocesan priest for the last thirty-five years in a variety of settings. I have been a home missionary, a country pastor and a cathedral rector. I have preached in hundreds of parishes. I have conducted 55 parish missions. I served as a vocation director for seven years. I have taught, and continue to teach, in a seminary. I have read all the recent documents on this subject, and I have written a book for seminarians on becoming members of their presbyterates. Out of these experiences, I offer this small book and its insights to those of you who are making the transition out of the seminary and into diocesan priesthood in hopes that it will be of some help, and at least help you know what to expect. Knowing what to expect, you will hopefully be more prepared to manage the process successfully.

Warning! Priesthood is not for cowards or the faint of heart. Those who crave the security and comfort of a pedestal or who are merely content to play a role need not apply. It takes faith, humility and inner strength to act *in persona Christi*, especially in today's Church. In the end, priesthood is about having the zeal of an apostle in laying down one's life for God's people, in good times as well as in bad times.

The path of priesthood is a hero's journey, a quest. The struggle to discover the internal strength to sustain an external quest pervades all great traditions of mythology, folklore and legend.

This struggle is also the heart of the journey for spiritual leaders throughout the world. It is common for great spiritual leaders to undergo multiple internal and external tests of faith and discipline as they seek to achieve their goals of compassionate service to others and mastery of themselves. On a quest, there are dragons to be slain, mountains to climb, deserts to conquer, river to cross and storms to weather, both inside and out. Those serious about such quests know this and press on. Cowards are surprised and flee.

These "internal and external tests of faith and discipline" are also part of Christian discipleship, especially for those who carry on the ministry of the apostles. When Peter argued with Jesus (Matthew 16: 21-25), telling Jesus to quit all that talk about suffering to come, Jesus called Peter a "Satan," reminding him that "If a man wishes to come after me, he must deny his very self, take up his cross and begin to follow in my footsteps."

Peter became a model of those new to discipleship who are all talk when he said, "Though all may have their faith in you shaken, mine will never be shaken." Even when Jesus predicted that Peter would deny him three times, Peter still bragged, "Even though I have to die with you, I will never disown you." As the first disciples learned quickly, and every great saint since, it is one thing to pledge one's life to a high purpose, but it is another thing to carry through on that pledge.

When I was pastor of the Cathedral of the Assumption in Louisville from 1983-1997, I had the honor of living in the rectory with Archbishop Thomas C. Kelly, OP. After breakfast, he often left the kitchen with these words: "Well, I'm off to fight the forces of evil!" From the look on his face when he arrived home for dinner, it was obvious that he did not win every battle. But, no matter what, like scores of other bishops and priests today, he set out faithfully every morning to engage "the enemy."

This little book is written to encourage today's heroes, the newly ordained who are setting out on the quest of diocesan priesthood in today's contentious Church. This is not a pious little book about the glories of priesthood, written from some ivory tower. It is written by a priest who has been in the trenches for several years now.

Warning! In this book, I talk more about weathering storms than about basking in the calm, not because I am a pessimist, but because I believe some serious honesty will be more useful at this major transition point.

On the other hand, if I were only to speak of the problems that newly ordained priests will face, then this book would be of little value if it did not include advice on how to overcome those problems. As Johnny Sain once said, "Nobody wants to hear about the labor pains. They just want to see the baby." I am definitely an optimist about the future of priesthood, but there is great value, I believe, in speaking candidly about how to overcome the problems inherent in today's priesthood. Hopefully, there is some wisdom here, born of experience, that will help others new to the priestly path.

The bottom line for me and for the other 90% of all American priests is that we are happy and that we would certainly do it again, in spite of the many difficulties that surround being a priest today. To borrow the words of an old gospel song, the big majority of us "wouldn't take nothin' for our journey now." In their names, I welcome you, our about-to-be-ordained, to the quest. In the words of St. Theresa, "Anyone who realizes that he or she is favored by God will have the courage necessary for doing great things."

As for me, I love being a priest. I always have, and I hope I always will. However, I am not leaving it to chance. I am dedicated, with God's help, to "cultivating my own garden." I highly recommend that you commit to doing the same. Do not leave your happiness and effectiveness as a priest to luck or to others. God certainly helps those who are committed to helping themselves.

*Rev. J. Ronald Knott, Director*
*Institute for Priests and Presbyterates*
*Saint Meinrad School of Theology*
*St. Meinrad, Indiana 47577*
*Feast of the Holy Innocents, December 28, 2004*

# CHANGE: THE FIRST OF MANY

*The only constant in life is change.*
Francois de la Rochefoucald

The transition from seminary into priestly ministry is similar to leaving home, graduating from school, beginning a career, getting married and starting a family – all at once.[1]

The departure from seminary and entry into priestly ministry, while usually a highly anticipated event and a greatly welcomed one, is often an occasion of some unconscious grieving over what was left behind and conscious anxiety over what lies ahead. This transition marks a move from the predictable routine of student status into an uncertain place in the midst of a new set of established co-workers and daily tasks, from the development and formation of oneself as a seminarian to a centering in service and mission to others as an ordained priest.

Even though the identity of the newly ordained priest is conferred in ordination, it may not be fully and consciously appropriated for some time. This transition can be accompanied by disillusionment, struggle and even crisis. Often this occurs within the first three to eighteen months. Sometimes it represents a brief moment; other times it is more protracted. We are learning the hard way that not enough attention is being paid to this initial transition.

The transition from seminarian to priest is the first of many in the life of a priest. The initial transition is followed by one transition after another: from parochial vicar to first pastorate, from first pastorate to another and then another, from young adulthood to midlife, and finally from midlife into what has been called "the third age," ages 65-95 and sometimes beyond that.

The tasks and challenges of all these transitions can be clustered around the basic movements of departing, entering, settling in and departing again. Each transition combines challenges that are both psychological and spiritual. "The birds of the air have nests, but the Son of Man has nowhere to lay his head."

In Scripture, the story of the Exodus offers us a helpful map for the process of transition, be it the Church in general or priests and others in particular. The Exodus paradigm seems to have four movements: a setting out in excitement, a period of disillusionment, a call to perseverance and, finally, a time of integration.

When Moses led the people out of Egypt toward the Promised Land, they left with images of milk and honey dancing in their heads. Not too long into their journey, they hit a desert – a place of hunger, thirst and danger; an unfamiliar place of uncertainty and doubt. Worn out and losing hope, they complain and yearn for the good old days. They want to go back to what was familiar. Moses, who had the duty of keeping hope alive, keeps prodding them to go on. Finally, after forty years of wandering, they see the Promised Land on the horizon and finally move into it.

Setting out in excitement, a period of disillusionment, a call to perseverance and a time of integration are part of every transition, be it remodeling a house, the path to sobriety, a new marriage, an abused spouse leaving the abuser, a Church in the process of renewal, a seminarian becoming a priest or a priest moving through assignments. "With each passage of human growth, we must shed a protective structure (like a hardy crustacean). We are left exposed and vulnerable – but also yeasty and embryonic again, capable of stretching in ways we hadn't known before." (Gail Sheehy)

To every seminarian about to become a priest, I say this, "Expect a desert! It's part of the deal." When you hit that desert, and you will, do not conclude that you have made a mistake. Conquer your desert, and by conquering it, you will be even more prepared and more suited for priestly ministry. Then, after you have conquered several of your own, you will have the know-how to lead others through their deserts.

## DISCUSSION STARTERS

1. Recall the major transitions you have experienced so far in your life. Which ones happened to you, and which ones did you consciously choose? Did you feel powerless or powerful?

2 What are the major changes that will occur in your life in the near future, and what plans do you have to deal with them?

3. What do you think will be the hardest adjustment you will need to make?

4. To whom can you go if you experience difficulty, and why do you think they will be able to help?

5. How can what you've learned about handling change help others who undergo change, either by choice or by circumstance?

# DECIDING TO GROW UP

*The Spirit God gave us is no cowardly spirit, but rather one*
*that makes us strong, loving and wise.*
II Timothy 1:7

It's time for straight talk. The transition from seminarian to priest requires, above all, a conscious decision to grow up. "When I was a child, I used to talk like a child, think like a child, reason like a child. When I became a man I put childish ways aside." (I Corinthians 13:11)

When I was going from parish to parish, at home and around the country, preaching missions, retreats and days of recollection to fallen-away Catholics, and especially when I traveled around speaking on religious vocations as a vocation director, I got an ear full on what Catholics want from priests. My sense is that lay people are weary of immaturity, bad service, incompetence and an inability to lead. They may have allowed us to get away with those things in the past, but no more. Lay people today, more than ever, expect and deserve competent pastors with the ability to elicit from and coordinate the charisms of lay people.

Somebody besides Father Andrew Greeley ought to be saying it: The last thing the Church today needs is yet another needy, immature little boy in a Roman collar who could not make it in the real world. There are enough absurd caricatures who have all the trappings of priesthood but lack the capacity to function as effective priests. We already have too many priests who see their ordinations as guaranteeing them the right to enter parishes as if those parishes were their personal feudal benefices, entitling them to be taken care of for the rest of their lives no matter how bad the service rendered, or the immature, inept and inane believe that a Roman collar will guarantee them respect without having to earn it. Lay people today are tired, as well, of "feverish little clods of grievances and ailments, always whining that the Church will not get together to make them happy," to paraphrase George Bernard Shaw.

Robert Bly is the author of "The Sibling Society," a book about "a culture where adults remain children and where children have no desire to become adults." Michael Ventura and James Hillman are co-authors of *We've Had 100 Years of Psychotherapy and the World's Getting Worse.* They say that adolescence today lasts from early teens to late middle age.

The culture of "perpetual adolescence" is effecting both marriage and priesthood, the sacraments geared toward the salvation of others. The high divorce rate among married people and the high drop-out rate among the newly ordained may be the result of people who refuse to grow up, making serious commitments that effect others and that they are emotionally and spiritually unable to keep.

What lay people want, and deserve, are competent, mature spiritual leaders who are good and also good at what they do. They want faith-filled, compassionate, down-to-earth men of integrity and competence to lead them and inspire them, not little demagogues, lacking in ability, self-control and personal discipline, who lord it over them. Andrew Greeley says they are "sloppy in their professional activities and contemptuous of their laity." The laity want articulate spiritual guides who can "walk the talk." They want priests who can preach well, pray well and lead well – and yes, they also want a little kindness at the door, on the phone and in the office.

Lay people want their priests, in the words of Saint Paul to Timothy, to be "strong, loving and wise."

## STRONG

In his second letter to the young missionary Timothy, Paul is writing to a scared young man. Timothy was undertaking an apparently impossible task, was facing the opposition of both Church and state, and was feeling overwhelmed by his own fear of failure. Paul reminds Timothy that the Spirit will give him *dunymis*, *agape* and *sophronismos*, making him strong, loving and wise.

*Dunymis* is translated as strength. Here it means *strength* in the sense of *adequacy to meet life effectively, the strength to do well what needs to be done.*

Priests have a triple role in the Church: preachers of the Word, presiders at the celebration of the sacraments and leaders of the community. They are not the only leaders, but leaders nonetheless.

People want strength from their priests, not authoritarianism. Authoritarianism dismisses the rightful role of others as also responsible for carrying out some part of Christ's work, given to them at baptism. Priests today must remember that when authority is duly exercised, it is done not so much to command as to serve.

Abdication of authority is equally destructive to the Church. Some priests have assumed that encouraging lay ministry means the abdication of their pastoral authority, allowing all manner of craziness (their own and well as that of others) to fill the vacuum. Rather, as Pope John Paul II tells us in *I Will Give You Shepherds*, the more lay ministry develops the more need there is for holy and effective priests. One of the roles of a priest is to guard the common good of the community. To do that, he must not only have a personal point of view, but must move regularly to a viewing point. From there he can appreciate his own point of view as well as that of others.

A *strong* leader is one who has integrity, discipline, courage and confidence and who can inspire the same in others.

## LOVING

*Agape*, translated as *love*, is not merely a sentimental feeling toward people. It means *practical helpfulness.* Good will and warm feelings are not enough for those who would be pastors of today's parishes. Practical helpfulness, competence if you will, is the loving service that people need from their leaders in the Church.

# WISE

Sophronismos, a difficult to translate Greek word, means self-control, prudence, temperance or moderation. Being a naïve loose cannon, especially under pressure, is a menacing quality in a pastoral leader. Unable to control himself in trying times, how can he possibly be able to guide others through their moments of panic and trial? Being calm, cool and collected and maintaining grace under pressure are qualities that will be called on many times in pastoral ministry.

---

## DISCUSSION STARTERS

1. What do you look forward to most as a priest? What do you dread most as a priest?

2. What does the Church teach about the relationship of ordained ministry to lay ministry?

3. What does being an authority figure mean to you?

4. Whom do you know in the priesthood who most exhibits the qualities of being strong, loving and wise? How so?

5. Which of these three qualities do you feel personally most confident about?

6. Which of these qualities do you feel will need more personal development?

---

# WHAT KIND OF PRIEST DO YOU WILL TO BE?

*Love is patient; love is kind. Love is not jealous; it does not put on airs,it is not snobbish. Love is never rude; it is not self-seeking; it is not prone to anger; neither does it brood over injuries. Love does not rejoice in what is wrong but rejoices in the truth. There is no limit to love's forbearance, to its trust, its hope, its power to endure. There are in the end three things that last: faith, hope, and love, and the greatest of these is love.*
I Corinthians 13:4-7,13

By ordination, you will be a priest and you will always be a priest. That is a given. You have not only been called to priesthood in general, you have also been called to be either a diocesan priest or a religious priest. When a call to priesthood is coupled with an attraction to being with the people of God in a given place and serving them particularly in parish ministry, then the call points to diocesan priesthood.

As a diocesan priest, you have been called forth from the laity to live among the laity and to focus your ministry on the mission and spirituality of the laity. For most diocesan priests, this means being a pastor of a parish. As a religious priest, you have been called to take vows, serve, live and pray in community, following the rule and living the charism of the order of which you are a member. Some religious priests work with diocesan priests as members of presbyterates, as long as they are in the diocese, as pastors, associate pastors and in other diocesan ministries.

Now that you will to be a diocesan priest, what *kind* of priest do you *will* to be? Your family history, your personality type, your pastoral experience or lack of it, your seminary's perspective, what you chose to accept or reject in your formation, will all affect the shape of your priesthood in various conscious and unconscious ways. Whether they admit it or not, all priests are cafeteria priests, picking and choosing from the volumes of theology on priesthood and from the many models they have met, to assemble *their* version of priesthood, even those who swear to be true followers of the magisterium.

Shall I be like Archbishop Oscar Romero or Cardinal Joseph Bernardin, Pope John Paul II or Pope John XXIII, St. John Vianney or Fr. Andrew Greeley, Fr. Phillip Berrigan or Fr. Benedict Groeschel, the pastor I grew up with or the pastor I spent my deacon summer with? Shall I obey the Pope, but not my Bishop? Shall I be involved in abortion issues, but not capital punishment issues; liturgical issues, but not ecumenical and interfaith issues? Shall I honor the Council of Trent, but not Vatican II? Can I work only in the city, but not the country; only with nuns in habits, but not those in street clothes; only with men and not women; only with conservatives, but not liberals?

Now that you will be a priest, what kind of priest do you *choose* to be? Do you even know *why* you choose what you choose? Do you understand how your own experience has shaped the choices you are making? Can you reverence the choices of other priests that may lead them to a different option than yours?

There is an old fable about six blind men and an elephant that might fit here.

## The Parable of the Blind Men and the Elephant
**(John Godfrey Saxe's [1816-1887] version of the famous Indian legend)**

It was six men of Indostan
To learning much inclined,
Who went to see the Elephant
Though all of them were blind,
That each by observation
Might satisfy his mind.
The First approached the Elephant

24

And, happening to fall
Against his broad and sturdy side,
At once began to bawl:
"God bless me, but the Elephant
Is very like a wall!"

The Second, feeling the tusk,
Cried, "Ho! what have we here
So very round and smooth and sharp?
To me 'tis very clear
This wonder of an Elephant
Is very like a spear!"

The Third approached the animal
And, happening to take
The squirming trunk within his hands,
Thus boldly up he spake:
"I see," quoth he, "The Elephant
Is very like a snake!"

The Fourth reached out an eager hand,
And felt about the knee:
"What most the wondrous beast is like
Is very plain," quoth he;
"'Tis clear enough the Elephant
Is very like a tree!"

The Fifth, who chanced to touch the ear,
Said, "Even the blindest man
Can tell what this resembles most;
Deny the fact who can:
This marvel of an Elephant
Is very like a fan!"

The Sixth no sooner had begun
About the beast to grope
Than, seizing on the swinging tail

That fell within his scope,
"I see," quoth he, "the Elephant
Is very like a rope!"

And so these men of Indostan
Disputed loud and long,
Each in his own opinion
Exceeding stiff and strong.
Though each was partly in the right,
They all were in the wrong!

We all touch the truth, but none of us experiences the whole truth. The Church has "the Truth," but individually we experience only part of that great Truth. That is why the "eye cannot say to the ear, I don't need you!" As Catholics, our charism is to hold a variety of experiences of the truth together in one big Truth. As a pastor and promoter of the common good, you will not have the luxury of merely having a point of view. You will have to appreciate and negotiate many points of view. Embrace truth, but always in its depth.

The problem is not with the truth, but one's perception, grasp and understanding of truth. Some people confuse their conviction, zeal and passion for a certain position with the truth itself. "If I am this sure, then it must be true." One only has to think of those in the Church in bygone days who were convinced that the earth was flat and that the sun revolved around the earth. Their certainty, and rigid defense of that certainty, did not make it true. Before his conversion, when he was still Saul, Paul refers to himself as a "staunch defender of God" when he was on his crusade to eliminate the followers of "this new way." He arrested both men and women who were followers of Jesus. He even went to Damascus to arrest Christians and bring them back to Jerusalem for punishment. A righteous young Saul stood watch over the clothes of those who stoned Stephen to death. Acts 8:1 says that "Saul entirely approved of the killing." It took God to knock him off his "high horse."

Arrogant certainty, combined with ignorance, always spells disaster.

With all that said, there are types of priests you may want to emulate and types you may want to avoid imitating.

## THE PRIEST THAT PEOPLE WANT

Priests are, first of all, weak human beings. No one is really worthy of this vocation, but God has always chosen the weak and made them strong in bearing witness to him. The apostles were weak: Peter denied Jesus, Judas betrayed him, and the rest abandoned him in his darkest hour, with the exception of John. Yet all but Judas were strengthened by the Holy Spirit and became great saints.

Lay people need to know that the validity of the message does not depend on the goodness of the messenger. The unworthiness of the priest does not prevent Christ from acting. As St. Augustine put it: Christ's gift is not profaned by a weak minister. What flows through him keeps its purity, and what passes through him remains clear. What passes through defiled human beings is not itself defiled.

With that said, Pope John Paul II may have best described the priest that people want when he wrote, "In order that his ministry may be humanly as credible and acceptable as possible, it is important that the priest should mold his human personality in such a way that it becomes a bridge and not an obstacle in their meeting with Jesus Christ."[2]

To be bridges and not obstacles, people want their priests to be whole, holy and effective. They want them to be parables of Christian discipleship. "We need heralds of the Gospel who are experts in humanity, who have shared to the full the joys and sorrows of our day, but who are, at the same time, contemplatives in love with God."[3]

Healthy and happy priests[4] are realistically oriented, spontaneous, accepting of themselves and others. They are problem solvers, autonomous and independent, creative, humorous, nonconforming, positive and sincere.

If they function well, they are risk takers, confident and enthusiastic, integrated and congruent, self-directive and self-actualizing. They are people with high esteem who generally accept the way life treats them. They are active participants rather than reactive receptors. Far from fearing change, they welcome it and know that it is an inescapable part of life. Healthy priests have made the decision to embrace challenges and change, and they see them as life-giving. They have a sense of unity and balance in their lives.

Healthy priests maintain a realistic sense about complex demands, make wise choices about how to use their time and are able to see the whole picture without losing touch with the details. Their honesty enables them to keep a sense of vision and passion for mission.

Happy priests enjoy being accountable to others and want the same from them. Well-adjusted priests have learned to find support and meet their needs for appropriate intimacy in a variety of healthy ways.

These priests are believers in God and in themselves. They believe that what they are doing is worthwhile, that the Good News is **the** important message for the world, and they wait for the coming of the kingdom in God's good time.

Holy priests maintain their relationship with Jesus by engaging in spiritual practices: prayer, Scripture reading and study, and the celebration of the liturgy. Effective priests practice the constant awareness of the presence of God in their lives. They believe God is actively involved in their lives and ministry, that God is working through them and that they receive back more than they give in doing ministry.

# THE "PROPHET" PRIEST

The Church today has many great prophets. Some are priests and some are not, some are Catholic and some are not, some are individuals and some are groups. Some of these prophets and prophetic groups speak **in the name of** the Church and some speak **to** the Church.

Prophets are not so much people who predict the future as they are people who make us see what is going on in the present, what is under our very noses, the things that we would rather not see. As such, they are people of insight more than people of foresight. Prophets come in a variety of packages.

Pope John Paul II and the National Conference of Catholic Bishops have certainly been prophetic in their encyclicals and pastoral letters on war, the economy, abortion and capital punishment, to name a few. Mother Teresa of Calcutta has been a prophet, raising our consciousness to the plight of the poorest of the poor.

Not every priest who speaks out forcefully is a prophet. Some self-styled prophets are just angry people who love to work out their unresolved personal issues under the umbrella of a "ministry of rage," offering more fury than light and never meeting an authority figure, woman, liberal or conservative they didn't hate. Other self-styled prophets have grown to resemble the mean God their minds have created, offering nothing more than a lifetime of "sinners in the hands of an angry God" speeches. They never meet a person who doesn't need to be condemned for something or other.

Nasty, angry, judgmental and hateful are not synonyms for prophetic. Unlike a true prophet who speaks the truth with love, they merely like to hear themselves rant and rave, thinking they can demonstrate their commitment by forcing commitment onto others. A firm conviction that a thing is so does not necessarily make it so.

Zealots tend to be single-issue people. In the long run of history, the censor and the inquisitor have always lost. The only sure weapon against bad ideas is better ideas. The best pastors are those who ignore zealots of every sort and listen to the less shrill voices of reason.

## THE "LEVELER" PRIEST

"Anything you can do, I can do better." Jealousy and competitiveness have been the dark side of clerical culture for a very long time, probably from the beginning. When the apostles, James and John, were caught making a move to grab the best seats in Jesus' new kingdom, they had to face the indignation of the other ten apostles as well as a stern reprimand from Jesus.

The *Basic Plan for the Ongoing Formation of Priests* dedicates quite a bit of space to the subject of clerical envy and competition. Whether you like his work or not, Father Andrew Greeley makes a good point in his book, *Priests: A Calling in Crisis* (pp. 107-108). He talks about the leveling that goes on in presbyterates, whereby priests are reluctant to applaud the work of other priests for fear that it will take away something from themselves.

He says that, in the clerical culture, "to be a member of good standing, a priest must try not to be too good at anything or to express unusual views or criticize accepted practices or even to read too much. Some ideas are all right, but too many ideas are dangerous." "When a layman mentions that Father X is a good preacher, the leveler priest's response might likely be, 'Yes, he preaches well, but he doesn't get along with kids.'" Or, "He's really good, but all he does during the week is prepare his sermon." Or, "everyone says that, and it's probably true, but he's not an easy man to live with."

# THE "AMBIVALENT" PRIEST

"No one who puts his hand to the plow and then keeps looking back is fit for the kingdom of God." Some priests spend their whole priesthood in a perpetual identity crisis, always looking back, looking around or second-guessing the decision they have made. Rather than looking for good reasons to stay, they are always looking for reasons to quit and give up. With a divided heart, they are physically in and emotionally out, spending more time questioning their call than they do minding their call.

Jesus may have said it best: "Remember, where your treasure is, there your heart is also. No man can serve two masters. He will either hate one and love the other or be attentive to one and despise the other" (Matthew 6: 21, 24). The word decision means to cut in two, meaning something is embraced and something is rejected. A priest must focus on what has been embraced and practice custody of the eyes and heart when it comes to what was left behind.

## THE "CLIMBER" PRIEST

When I was a seminarian, "the man with the plan" was said to have scarlet fever. This disease manifested itself in an inordinate desire to wear the color fuschia. Having designs on being a bishop, he was the one who always said the right thing, who was always to be found in the right place at the right time, who always got behind the right outrage, who always did the expected thing. He was the type to become a member of the Canon Law Society as a seminarian. He chose the "right" seminary, was the first in line to profess loyalty to the Holy Father and knew all the American bishops' names and ordination dates by heart. He knew the names of some of the most obscure clerical vesture, and if the truth be known, had a zuchetto in his sock drawer, just in case of an emergency.

Liberal? Conservative? He could become whatever was expedient. At the heart of this lust for power is a failure to understand that true power in the Church derives from the ability to make other people powerful. It is not so much to command as to serve. Proper authority is a gift to the Church, not to the one exercising it. He fails to realize the basic truth of leadership in today's Church: "Heavy hangs the head that wears the crown."

## THE "PERPETUAL ADOLESCENT" PRIEST

There are priests who are frozen in perpetual adolescence. They are the types who tend to buy Jeep Wranglers, flashy red convertibles and motorcycles with their ordination gifts. They are the ones who take too many vacations, each time coming back with a new hair color, body piercing or tattoo. They are the ones who seek out, and can only function in, youth ministry, not to meet the needs of youth but to meet their own needs. Distracted, unfocused and bleeding emotionally, they are unable to carry through or get organized, even if their lives depended on it. Oblivious to how obvious they are to others, these sad priests are potentially dangerous to themselves and those they are called to serve.

## THE "GOOD-OLD-BOY" PRIEST

Some priests think it is macho to be rude and crude, both in their personal habits and in their relationships with others. It can come from a conscious reaction to the "prissiness" of some priests or simply from being a single male for too long. They think sexist jokes and remarks are funny. Focusing only on themselves, they think being inappropriately dressed for formal occasions is a mark of independence or manliness. They believe that being unshaven and disheveled for public events is a sign of being down-to-earth and "with the people." In the end, they fail to accept the dictum that "there is a time and a season for every purpose under heaven." In the end, they fail to realize that we are not so much independent as we are interdependent. We do not operate in a vacuum. We operate in relationship with others.

# THE "MOLE" PRIEST

*(The Pharisees) kept an eye on Jesus ... hoping to be able to bring an accusation against him. When they went outside, they immediately began to plot with the Herodians how they might destroy him.*
– Mark 3: 2, 6

A little knowledge is a dangerous thing. Fidelity to the Church matters, but such fidelity does not constitute a license to operate as a one-man Inquisition. There are some priests who think they have been given the job of secret agent man – sniffing out heresy and denouncing it; indulging in simplistic labeling, categorizing and denouncing those who disagree with them; seeking out and banding together with like-minded people to engage in character assassination in the name of half-truths. They "put people to death while claiming to be serving God" (John 16:2).

Like the white-washed tombs that Jesus talked about, they look good on the outside but inside are filled with stench, presenting a holy exterior while hypocrisy and evil fill them within. They are wolves in sheep's clothing!

# THE "MOTHER-MAY-I" PRIEST

Respect for legitimate authority is a good trait in priests, but a childish dependence and inability to make ordinary decisions without parental approval is to be shunned whenever possible. This kind of priest is constantly calling, writing to and tying up the Chancery staff with trivialities, special requests and clarifications.

# THE "SAVIOR" PRIEST

A few priests are workaholics. In a misguided attempt to single-handedly "fill up in their own flesh what is lacking in the sufferings of Christ for the sake of his body, the Church" (Colossians 1:24), they drive themselves to the point of exhaustion and bad health. Here St. Charles Borromeo has some practical wisdom. "Are you exercising the care of souls? Do not thereby neglect yourself. Do not give yourself to others to such an extent that nothing is left of yourself for yourself. You should certainly keep in mind the souls, but without forgetting yourself."

For the bridge between God and his people to be worthy, the bridge must be maintained.

# THE "PRIVATE PRACTICE" PRIEST

As a way to cope with the complexity of being a priest in today's Church, either because of not wanting to deal with differing ecclesiologies or because of having to change familiar habits, some priests have emotionally dropped out. They never go to meetings, never serve on diocesan committees, never collaborate with other priests. They go into what one priest called "private practice." This isolation goes against all that a diocesan priest is said to be, both in Canon Law, the Council and the teaching of the American bishops.

Canon Law (245, no. 2) says that seminary students are to be so formed that they are prepared for fraternal union with the diocesan presbyterate. The Council says that no priest can, in isolation or single-handedly, accomplish his mission in a satisfactory way. He can do so only by joining forces under the direction of Church authorities. *The Basic Plan for the Ongoing Formation of Priests* (NCCB) notes that priests are not priests one by one, but serve the Church in a presbyterate. Priests are meant to work as a team, even when they do different work and live in different locations.

# THE PRIEST OF HOPE

In the spirit of Isaiah, priests who are "parables of hope" have an inner peace that no storm can shake. People are drawn to them like moths to a flame. Isaiah was the eternal optimist in the midst of warfare and corrupt religious and political leadership. Isaiah could sit on a pile of rubble and say, "This, too, will be rebuilt!" He could look at a barren desert and proclaim that "The desert will bloom, and streams of water will gush throughout the barren land."

In a tumultuous world, people need to have priest-leaders who have a peaceful center that no storm can shake.

---

## DISCUSSION STARTERS

1. Name some priests you admire and hope to emulate. What is it about them that inspires you?

2. Name some priests who operate out of an ecclesiology that seems to differ from yours. What is it about them that causes you to distance yourself from them? How can you reverence and respect their work?

3. How will you relate to parishioners who have ecclesiologies different from yours?

4. Which of the various types listed above do you most want to avoid?

5. Now that you will be a priest, what kind of priest do you will to be?

6. Describe yourself as the priest as you would hope to be on your 25th anniversary.

---

# WHEN IDEALS AND
# REALITY MEET

*When the going gets tough, the tough get going.*
Joseph P. Kennedy

If only ordination guaranteed that we would automatically live happily ever after! Obviously, it doesn't! Plan on the fact that it doesn't, and prepare yourself to be responsible for your own happiness. At ordination, you will be a priest, a priest forever, but whether you will be a happy and effective priest will depend on you.

Seminaries tend to deal in ideals, and rightly so, but ideal situations seldom exist in the messy world of today's parishes. Therefore, some advice not only on how to survive, but also on how to thrive, in the real world of pastoral ministry in today's Church might be helpful.

When I was in my last semester of seminary, one of my teachers in pastoral practice offered us a practical model on how to approach our work in the real world of priestly ministry. He would give us a pastoral situation and then ask us what the best way would be to approach that situation. After we came up with a list of ideal solutions, he asked us to tear them up, saying, "You'll probably never get a chance to do that, so *now* what can you do?"

This idea has been the most beneficial idea I took from the time we spent in pastoral formation class. In my 35 years of priesthood, I have used it over and over again. It was helpful when I had to decide to accept my first assignment to a place every bone in my body wanted to reject. It was helpful when I went to a rural parish known for its resistance to change. It was helpful when I accepted the challenge to revitalize a center-city cathedral parish with a handful of people and very little money. It was helpful again when I was vocation director during the abuse scandal when the pickings were already slim. The trick, of course, is to see possibilities where no one else sees them, to find the silver lining in clouds and to see opportunities even in disappointment and lack of resources.

"The bishop should..." "The Chancery is supposed to..." "Parishioners ought to..." "Other priests are supposed to..." Maybe they should, but what if they *don't?* Life is not always fair. People don't always do as they should. Systems fail. When people and systems fail you – and believe me, they will – learn to take charge. Powerlessness is a learned trait, but so is resourcefulness.

It is hard enough being a priest if you have a perfect assignment, a comfortable rectory, a big budget, a large staff, a beautiful church, a great support system and everybody worshiping the ground you walk on. But what do you do when you get an awful assignment, when your living space is small and lacks privacy, when the parish is broke and woefully understaffed, when the church is ugly and in need of repair, when your support system is miles away and when respect for priesthood has been all but destroyed by the bad behaviors of a series of priests before you? What you do in situations like these will either make or break you as a priest. People disappoint. Systems fail. Things are not always as they should be. Get used to it, and learn to deal constructively with it. A problem bigger than the number of priests is the lack of imagination among priests.

## MORALE

Back in the 1980s, the American bishops issued a document on priest morale. It defined morale as "an internal state of mind with regard to hope and confidence." In what I think is the most significant insight of the document, the writers point out that morale is ultimately the responsibility of the individual priest.

This document twice calls for heroic virtue in dealing with the reality of being a priest in a Church in transition. I read somewhere, years ago, that when all aspects of belief are in serious turmoil (partly because the pressures of our age are so hostile toward belief and partly because preservers of the status quo are so entrenched), heroic discipline is required of those who try to maintain a vital connection with today's broken world and the spiritual claims of the past.

It's hard to be a priest in a Church in transition. When old forms are failing miserably, even when they cannot handle the problems of today, they are fiercely defended. Under the pressure of disintegrating norms, a few propose new pathways. At first there is a traditionalist backlash who urge a restatement of the old norms, but eventually, out of necessity, the new ideas prevail, are adopted, and the Church moves into a new era. We are not there yet, and so heroic virtue is required. You can measure a man by the opposition it takes to discourage him.

## WHAT YOU DON'T KNOW CAN HURT YOU

Seminaries are doing a good job, but they cannot do it all. It would be ideal if seminaries could teach all that priests need to know in a typical seminary program, but they *do not* because they *cannot*. Ongoing formation needs to relieve the pressure on already overtaxed seminaries.

There are many things about being a priest that one can only learn through experience and reflection on that experience. Sadly, this kind of learning is, for all intents and purposes, *elective* in most dioceses. Ongoing formation has to be embraced by the individual priest. Those who have a passion for becoming an effective pastoral leader will find a way to become an effective pastoral leader, regardless of their pastoral situation and its limitations.

When I found myself, as a newly ordained priest, in the home missions of our diocese, it was obvious to me from day one that I was not prepared to do what I was being asked to do. I knew little about the Bible Belt culture, little about evangelism, fundamentalism, how to raise money, how to live alone or how to start a parish.

Like most seminarians, I was trained to be an associate pastor in an urban or suburban parish.

Even when I was ready to learn these things, money for ongoing education was not available in those days. Even if money had been available, I found out that appropriate programs to meet my needs were also not available in the Church. I could have toughed it out and made the most of it, but because I desperately wanted to learn the skills needed to do a good job, I decided to think outside the box. I applied to McCormick (Presbyterian) Seminary in Chicago to be a Doctor of Ministry student in their parish revitalization program. I solved the money problem by applying for a scholarship. Because of the smallness of my two mission churches and because I was the first Catholic priest to take up residence in those counties, I received a full scholarship on two grounds: poverty income and minority religion.

Today, with the time between ordination and first pastorate being shortened dramatically, ongoing formation, consciously and freely chosen by the individual priest, is an absolute necessity. As programs are being developed and refined, the individual priest must (a) develop an appetite for learning those skills that will make him effective and (b) be imaginative in finding the resources to meet that need.


# KNOW YOURSELF

*Know thyself!* – Socrates


If a priest is a bridge between God and his people, then the priest not only needs to know both ends of the bridge, but he must also know himself well. If the bridge is not sound, those who cross over it are endangered.

A priest who is not in touch with his own sexuality often projects his fears, obsessions and unresolved issues onto others. I remember one Protestant minister from the days when I was a newly ordained priest who used to rant and rave about other people's sexual morality almost daily on his radio program. He saw sexual immorality everywhere. His obsession culminated in a well-advertised event, a huge bonfire in front of his church.

40

He invited people to bring their TVs, dirty books and indecent clothes to be burned. A few days after the big bonfire production, he ran off with the church's teenaged organist! As St. Theresa of Avila said, "I don't fear the devil nearly as much as those who fear the devil."

Priests who come into pastoral leadership roles with unresolved parental issues often have authority issues as well. They are unable to be in an authority role appropriately or respect those who are in those roles. Unable to inspire people to greatness, these are the priests who rant and rave about how they ought to be listened to simply "because I am the pastor."

Old ecclesiologies and ecclesiastical garb are tempting shortcuts to status. The status of priests truly rises in the eyes of the laity when we priests really *priest*, when we really act *in persona Christi*. When we truly act *in persona Christi*, we are truly ambassadors for Christ. Pope John Paul tells us that we need to be "bridges, not barriers" to God.

Some priests do not know how to relate successfully to authority, keeping that balance between respect for authority and challenging authority appropriately. This assumes that the authority figure is comfortable and secure enough in his role to tolerate a frank discussion. Sometimes a bishop is wise enough to change his mind when priests have a valid point to make. But after arguing his point and losing, we diocesan priests are called to fall back on our promise of obedience, for the good of the Church.

Priests who grew up deprived of love and affection often cannot lead because of their insatiable appetite for being liked, approved of and appreciated. Their own neediness gets in the way of being able to freely give to others, to maintain boundaries and to do hard things when they need to be done. Without a constant supply of outside approval, these priests are prone to depression and unrealistic expectations.

From experience, I have concluded that the more people are torn up inside, the more they need things outside them to be nailed down. Being rigid, inflexible and judgmental as a priest is often presented as unwavering orthodoxy, when it may be nothing more than manifestations of pathological fear and an inability to cope with complexity.

Celibacy can be a heroic lifestyle for the healthy and well-adjusted person, but it can also be a hideout for misogyny, prejudice against women. If a priest is not in touch with his own feelings about women and is incapable of establishing appropriate, healthy relationships with women, he can be a menace in pastoral ministry. Some of the anger of the laity may be the result of priests' insensitivity to parishioners, especially to female parishioners. With women doing the lion's share of lay ministry in the Church, it is crucial that priests, especially today, have a healthy respect and appreciation for the gifts and talents of women and an ability to work with them as partners in ministry.

## LEADERSHIP

People want their priests, above all, to be spiritual leaders. Even though we are designated to be spiritual leaders, spiritual leadership skills are not automatically infused at ordination. We must dedicate ourselves to becoming real spiritual leaders, not just in name, but also in fact.

*Designated* leaders are not necessarily *real* leaders. Ordination makes you a *designated* leader, but whether you become a *real* leader is a matter of intention, skill and practice. Good will is not a substitute for competency. A priest must be *agathos*, morally good, but also *kalos*, good at what he does. Pope Celestine V, the only pope to resign this office, proved that holiness is not, of itself, a quality of leadership. He was a very holy man but a very weak pope.

A true leader develops the ability to unleash the power of the team. Vision, and its communication through word and deed, is what pastoral leadership is all about. Holding a vision and being able to communicate it; courage; enthusiasm; assertiveness; competence in theology and practice – all of these are essential ingredients in the make-up of effective pastoral leaders. "For if the trumpet give an uncertain sound, who shall prepare himself to the battle" (I Corinthians 14:8).

42

# BE YOUR OWN HERO

*The last time I saw him, he was walking down Lovers' Lane holding his own hand.* –Fred Allen

Amniotic people are always looking for others to lean on and make responsible for their success and happiness. Confident, self-possessed people know that no matter what comes along, they can figure out a solution.

Effective mentors are rare; great spiritual directors are in short supply; and good friends are hard to come by. If you can find all three and have them at your service, you are a rare priest indeed! What do you do when you can't find that effective mentor you need? What do you do when you can't find the perfect spiritual director to fit you? What do you do when your best friend lives in another state, another diocese or another town?

You can be your own mentor. You can be your own spiritual director, if need be. You can be your own best friend.

---

## DISCUSSION STARTERS

1.  How much idealizing of priesthood do you think is helpful, and how much do you think is counter-productive?

2.  What personal experience or skills do you have for dealing with disappointment?

3.  When have you had to be creative in a less-than-perfect situation? How did you feel? Where did you turn for help or assistance or support?

4.  How much of your happiness as a priest will be your responsibility?

5.  What support should you be able to expect as a priest? From whom? What if you don't get it?

6.  Name a time when you had to solve an important problem on your own. How did you do it?

7.  What parts of yourself are still a mystery to you? Do you know what is at the root of your major fears, prejudices and passions? How much power do they still have over you?

8.  What is the difference between being good and being good at something? What are the drawbacks of one without the other?

---

# FROM PRIVATE PERSON
# TO PUBLIC PERSON

*The life I live now is not my own; Christ is living in me.*
Galatians 2:20

One of the most dramatic changes that occurs when a young man makes the transition from being a seminarian to being a priest is moving from being the recipient of formation to being one in charge of forming a faith community, from focusing on one's own personal good to focusing on the common good.

The initial formation of the seminary is, by its very nature, self-focused. The seminary years are a time for individuals to form their own points of view through the trial and error of proposing, arguing and defending. When one becomes a priest, and especially when one becomes a pastor, things change. The individual priest-pastor no longer has the luxury of merely holding to his own point of view and dismissing all others. As a leader of leaders, he must begin to appreciate his own point of view among many other valid points of view, because the priest-pastor is guardian of the common good, not merely his own personal good. "Indeed, in building up the Church, the pastor always moves from a personal to a community dimension. He is never to be the servant of an ideology or of a faction."[5]

A seminarian might enjoy the traditional seminary sport of ridiculing and demeaning points of view other than his own, but once a public person, once a leader of the faith community, once a priest, this can be disastrous to his effectiveness as a spiritual leader. Once a priest, if he is to be a credible spiritual leader, he must learn to reverence the many acceptable points of view allowed by the Church, even those that are personally irritating.

As a public person, a priest's words and deeds have ramifications far beyond what they had when he was a seminarian. "The faithful in the parish and those who collaborate in various pastoral activities see, observe, feel and listen not only when the Word of God is preached but also when the liturgy is celebrated; when they are received in the parish office; when the priest eats and when he rests and they are edified by his temperance and sobriety; when they visit his home and they rejoice in his simplicity and priestly poverty; when they talk about him and discuss common interests and are comforted by his spiritual outlook, his courtesy and his behavior in treating humble people with priestly nobility."[6]

The faithful in the parish are also affected by his rigidity, hard-headedness, inability to listen, lack of courtesy, brashness, crudeness, judgmentalism, dishonesty, cronyism and mean spirit. As one who claims to act *in persona Christi*, these personal traits have a greater detrimental affect than they would otherwise.

In our culture, we often hear of people trying to separate their private lives from their public lives. St. Paul often argued against such thinking among early believers, insisting on the total integration of their faith with who they were and what they did.

Lay people have a God-given ability to spot a phony from a mile away. They intuitively recognize a wolf in sheep's clothing when they see one. They expect us to be who we claim to be. The priest, above all, must integrate who he is, what he says and how he acts. A priest is not just an anonymous person; he is also a public religious symbol, a living sacramental and, whether he likes it or not, a role model.

People expect more from priests. Maybe they sometimes expect too much. St. John Chrysostom, writing 1500 years ago, sympathizes with our dilemma:

> *The priest's shortcoming simply cannot be concealed. On the contrary, even the most trivial soon gets known. For as long as the priest's life is well regulated in every particular point, the intrigues cannot hurt him. But if he*

*should overlook some small detail, as is likely for a human being on his journey across the devious ocean of life, all the rest of his good deeds are of no avail to enable him to escape the words of his accusers. That small offense casts a shadow over the rest of his life. Everyone wants to judge the priest, not as one clothed in flesh, not possessing a human nature, but as an angel, exempt from the frailty of others.* [7]

---

## DISCUSSION STARTERS

1. As a seminarian, what points of view did your point of view clash with most regularly?

2. How did you deal with other seminarians who held points of view different than yours? Did you try to understand their points of view, seek common ground, avoid personal contact, or demean and ridicule them either in public or behind their backs?

3. What changes, if any, will you have to make when you become a public person, especially a pastor?

4. Have you had an experience yet where the effect of what you said or what you did seemed to have a broader impact than you expected, simply because you were a seminarian?

5. What groups and perspectives in the Church do you have the hardest time being comfortable with? Do you have any strategy, other than avoidance, to deal with them?

6. What does it feel like to be held to a higher standard?

---

# EXITING THE SEMINARY: ISSUES AROUND LEAVING

*And to make an end is to make a beginning.*
*The end is where we start from.*
T.S. Eliot, "Little Gidding"

## PREPARING TO LEAVE

Every transition begins with an ending. There is a lot of excitement and anticipation in the months and weeks leading up to an ordination to the priesthood, a sense of finally getting there. This excitement can blind some seminarians to the more often than not unconscious grieving involved in leaving a familiar world and entering a new one. In this chapter, attention will be paid to the often-overlooked process of leaving the seminary.

1. **When it comes time to leave the seminary, you can either consciously manage your transition or you can passively let it happen to you.**

How you manage endings, how you leave places and people, says a lot about you, whatever the circumstances. Managing your own successful transition into ministry begins with a conscious and deliberate effort to make a good exit. The first impression you make as you enter your new parish is important, but so is the last impression you make as you leave the seminary. If you don't know how to leave the seminary well, you probably won't know how to leave a parish well. Both exits need to be done with reverence and care.

It took a lot of people to get you through the seminary: vocation directors, seminary faculty and staff, cooks and janitors, benefactors and pastoral supervisors, to name a few. Some of these people played a big role, and some played a small role.

Some people you noticed and some you didn't. Some of these people you liked, and some you didn't like. Some helped you by agreeing with you, and some helped you by challenging you. Some you will see again, and some you will never see again. Before you get absorbed in the dynamics of your own transition out of the seminary, find a time and a way to express your gratitude to those who have brought you this far. Priests are notorious for their failure to acknowledge gifts. This is a sure way of killing the golden goose.

Make peace with, and forgive, your enemies. Harbor no grudges, and take no mental garbage with you as you leave the seminary. Let go of the irrational idea that everyone should have behaved perfectly, that everyone needed to like you, that everyone needed to approve of you and all of your needs should have been met. Do it for your own peace of mind. If for no other reason, do it because they could end up being your bishop or boss someday.

No institution is ideal. No seminary gets everything right. There are no perfect seminarians. Seminaries are merely institutions made up of flawed human beings who try to do their very best to assist you on the road to priesthood. Putting them down for their flaws says more about you than it does about them. Forgive them, forgive yourself, and move on.

Most seminaries are struggling to stay open and are generously subsidized by the people who operate them. They did not charge you their real cost. Hopefully, you will promote your seminary to others, but if you can't, the best policy may be, "if you can't say something nice, say nothing at all."

Take what is yours and leave what is not yours. Leave your borrowed home as good as you found it, if not better.

Take time to celebrate reaching your goal of ordination. Plan and enjoy an extended vacation, if possible. Rest your body, mind and spirit. Prepare yourself for the next phase of your transition, a phase that will take a lot of energy and focus.

## 2. The second phase of any transition is a time of feeling lost and disoriented.

The more centered you are on the inside, the more external chaos you can handle. People who are torn up on the inside have little ability to handle external messiness. Your ability to tolerate ambiguity and uncertainty will stand as a critical skill during this phase of the important transition from the old and familiar role of seminarian to the new and unfamiliar role as a diocesan priest.

As I have mentioned previously in this book, the changes you will face in the transition out of seminary into priesthood are deceptively complex. You will go through a major shift in, and sometimes even the loss of, significant relationships. You will go through a major change in home life, from group living in a large institution to living with one, maybe two, very busy priests, not of your choosing, in a parish rectory. You could quickly become one of the 25% to 30% of the 44,000 American priests who live alone. You will leave a highly structured and organized seminary life to a life of reacting to a daily onslaught of unplanned crises while trying to get your regular work done. Your sleeping and eating patterns will probably be regularly disrupted.

These feelings of being lost and disoriented are part of the process in any transition. The time of setting out in excitement is always followed by a time of discomfort, even disillusionment. This, too, shall pass. If you persevere during this time, you will reach a day when the new shall be old, when the unfamiliar will become familiar and when the uncomfortable becomes comfortable.

## 3. The third stage of any transition is beginning again.

Just when you have successfully made your transition and finally gotten comfortable, it will be time to move on to a new assignment, to begin anew, to make another transition and to go through the whole process again, and again, and again throughout your priesthood. Regular transitions are built into diocesan priesthood. It's part of the deal.

# PREPARING TO BEGIN

Just as how you manage an ending says a lot about you, how you mange a beginning says a lot about you as well. Two major issues of the last semester in seminary are planning your ordination and planning your Mass of Thanksgiving. How you approach these two events will tell the whole Church an awful lot about you.

A diocesan priest is called from the laity, to live among the laity to serve and empower the laity. Your ordination is not **your** ordination. The ordination of a diocesan priest belongs to the diocesan Church. You do not call yourself to ordination. The Church calls you to ordination. When I was vocation director of our diocese, I tried to make it abundantly clear that while candidates for ordination could be polled for ideas, the ordination belonged to the local diocesan Church. As such, the ordination should theologically reflect in a real way what the rite says, not the personal whims and tastes of those ordained.

It is customary for a newly ordained priest to celebrate a Mass of Thanksgiving in his home parish and the parishes in which he was a guest during formational pastoral assignments. Again, it is so telling to hear a newly ordained talk about **his** Mass of Thanksgiving. How a newly ordained priest plans the traditional Mass of Thanksgiving says volumes about him, his theology and his view of people.

Moving into a parish as a new priest, bringing in mostly seminary friends, changing local customs by introducing practices foreign to the local community, giving a judgmental homily of all that has gone before you, and kicking regular parish ministers to the curb for your Mass of Thanksgiving has to be one of the most discounting, self-defeating and arrogant moves possible. The message to the local congregation is that this is **my** mass and I will do it **my** way, because the way **I** do things is better than they way **you** have been doing them. It is clericalism at its worst. People may have to put up with it for a day, but believe me, they take note of it, and many will write you off as just another arrogant little cleric who has come to be served rather than to serve.

Unfortunately, many Masses of Thanksgiving are modeled on the worst aspects of modern American "queen for a day" weddings. I've even seen three-tiered cakes with a priest at the altar by himself on top. Just as these bride-centered weddings obscure the religious aspects of the Sacrament of Matrimony, a priest-centered Mass of Thanksgiving obscures the theology of ordained ministry.

When you plan the Mass of Thanksgiving it would be smart to remember that you are a **guest** presider in an established faith community. Put Jesus and the community you pray with, not yourself, at the center of your focus. Involve the local congregation. Use local ministers as much as possible. Celebrate *with* them and not merely *in front of* them. Your Mass of Thanksgiving may be the first time to publicly act *in persona Christi*. This celebration is a teaching moment. Resolve to use it well. As you were challenged at your deacon ordination, "Teach what you believe and practice what you teach."

## KNOW WHO YOUR FRIENDS ARE

When I was a vocation director, I became aware of "shadow vocation directors," a certain subgroup of priests who befriended and guided some of the soon-to-be or newly ordained outside the official formation programs of their dioceses and seminaries. The newly ordained are particularly vulnerable to the suspicious concern and interest of ecclesiastical patrons and idealogues. Reject being seduced into the polemics of polarization. Beware of those who would divide rather than unite, exclude rather than include. Stay in dialogue with the larger Church.

## DISCUSSION STARTERS

1. Recall your transition into the seminary. Do you remember the excitement of being accepted and how it was followed by feelings of being lost as you began seminary training? How did you feel? When did those feelings begin to be replaced with a feeling of belonging?

2. What loose ends and fence-mending do you need to deal with before you leave the seminary?

3. What can you do to show your appreciation to your vocation director, spiritual director, professors, seminary staff, etc.?

4. What letdowns do you expect to experience after ordination? What can you do now to prepare to deal effectively with them?

5. How will your Masses of Thanksgiving reflect your theology of priesthood? How will you involve the people of the parish in these celebrations? How can this be a teaching moment?

6. What is the difference between being welcomed into the presbyterate and being recruited into an ideological subgroup?

# ENTERING A PARISH

*Remove the sandals from your feet,*
*for the place you stand is holy ground.*
Exodus 3:5

Not every priest knows how to enter a parish. "Fools rush in where angels fear to tread." Some newly ordained priests, in their beginner's zeal and in their eagerness to use all they have learned, sometimes enter parishes like bulls in a china shop. I can still remember being embarrassed when I was referred to as "brash" in an article in our diocesan paper when I was about to be ordained. Brash means "lacking restraint and discernment to the point of arrogance." It is a perennial, all too common trait among the newly ordained.

In their impetuous mission to fix what is wrong, some newly ordained priests "use a hatchet to remove flies from people's foreheads." Like the well-intentioned weeders in the parable of the weeds among the wheat, they think they can tell weeds from wheat and are more than willing to get to work, only to find out – too late – that they were misguided. Sometimes their cocky boldness is merely silly, but sometimes they do irreparable harm to people and lose years of good will that might have made them effective sooner, rather than later. Many newly ordained are shocked, surprised and disappointed when they discover that their collar alone is not enough to carry the day when parishioners disagree and have other ideas.

Rule number one when it comes to entering a parish is this: It is *their* parish, not *yours*. It is holy ground. You must, therefore, take off your shoes. Stop! Look! Listen! Before you start judging, stereotyping and trying to fix people, let them tell you who they are, where they are coming from, how they feel about themselves and what is going on in their lives. Do it without judgment. Just listen. Take it in. If you do that, they will begin to trust you and then, and only then, will they themselves begin to listen to you.[8]

People really listen only when they can identify in some way with the person who is talking. If not, there is no real communication. This identification is absolutely essential to trust and credibility. If people cannot identify with you, they do not give you credibility or trust, no matter how much you think you have to give.

Who are these people? As a parish priest, you stand in the presence of people of every conceivable level of faith. You celebrate with people who are already giving their lives in service to their spouses, children, neighbors and fellow parishioners. You look at people who have been through years of old, experienced love and people filled with the wonder and excitement of fresh, young love. You are facing rich people and poor people, the well-off and the cast-off. You are being watched by the esteemed and the rejected. There are people before you who have been nurtured by the Church and people who have been hurt by the Church. But, most of all, you have people who are all touched by the uncertainty of life, sickness, suffering, dying, separation, loss, rejection, loneliness and alienation. And if you are truly *wise*, and not just *smart*, you will know that you cannot see into hearts and you will not evaluate people by externals, coming to judgmental conclusions concerning matters about which you know very, very little.

After 35 years of priesthood, you begin to notice what works and what doesn't. In no certain order, I offer a short list of attitudes you should carry into ministry from day one.

## WANT WHAT YOU GET

Seldom do priests get exactly what they want in their assignments. Therefore, it is important to learn how to make yourself want what you get. Even though a particular parish community may be assigned to you as a priest, you can hopefully decide to consciously choose that parish community as your own in the process. In every parish, but especially in rural and struggling parishes, you will need to let your parishioners know on a regular basis that you are happy, blessed and honored to be their priest.

One of the practices that has worked everywhere I have been assigned is greeting parishioners at the door of the church every Sunday and seeing them off at the door after Mass, in fair weather and foul. This has been the single most effective pastoral practice of all.

Another practice is making it a personal policy to regularly affirm parishioners in my homilies. You can't do that till you mean it. If you don't mean it yet, a change of heart might be in order. People know in their guts whether you like them or not. If they know you love them, they will hear your voice and follow you. If not, don't be surprised if your words fall on deaf ears.

## PAY ATTENTION TO INDIVIDUALS

One of the first things to slide with busy, over-extended pastors and associate pastors is the personal touch, that one-on-one attention that people need and respond to so positively. In a very small parish, it is relatively easy to know what's going on among your parishioners. In a huge parish, it is almost impossible.

One of the most effective ideas I have ever come up with to help me maintain a personal touch in a large parish is to recruit a volunteer to assist me in paying attention to individual parishioners. This volunteer's job is to skim the newspaper, committee minutes, school newsletters and any other sources of information on parishioners. It is his or her job to draft cards and letters of thanks, sympathy or congratulations for me to sign. As my eyes and ears, this person helps me pay attention to those I am sent to serve. It is so effective, it borders on magic.

As I have said before in this book, priests are notorious for not returning calls, following up on requests and expressing thanks for gifts. It may be necessary to recruit some help to get this done, but there is no excuse for not doing it.

# SPEAK THE TRUTH WITH LOVE

What parishes need desperately today are priests who are bridge builders, peacemakers, reconcilers and mediators of unity. Priests need to be able to deal constructively with diversity, pluralism, complexity, ambiguity, division and polarization. Those who would exercise leadership in the Church are called to be ministers of healing communion. The Church needs, especially today, priests whose words heal rather than wound, who express themselves with sensitivity for the dignity and worth of every person. Civility, as one priest said, is not just a civil virtue. The Church today needs civility badly, and nowhere more desperately than among its priests.

Even though a policy of encouragement and affirmation should be a priority among parish priests, there are times when a challenge is called for from the pastor, especially when the common good is threatened by a few. Even though such challenges are not easy or popular, they are the truly loving thing to do. The secret is to speak without anger, false judgment or recrimination. A good shepherd "speaks the truth with love."

The American bishops *(As One Who Serves)* tell us that "The style of leadership on the part of the priest is one of service. He is to be a servant to the People of God, holding them accountable for what they have been and can be. He serves them by calling forth leadership and coordinating ministries." Holding them accountable must be done with love and patience, never with anger or meanness.

# LET THEM TEACH YOU

Priests sometimes give the notion that they are the only ones with something to teach or give. As the main coordinator of charisms in the parish, a priest must acknowledge and affirm the many and varied gifts within the community. He must be open to being a student as well as to being a teacher. People take ownership of the mission of the parish when their talents, gifts and expertise are called on and used.

To do this, the priest must understand that his role is to empower others, to serve instead of being served. Pope John Paul II put it this way: "The priesthood is not an institution that exists alongside the laity or *above* it. The priesthood of bishops and priests, as well as the ministry of deacons, is *for* the laity, and precisely for that reason it possesses a ministerial character, that is to say, one of service."

In my experience, if you enter a parish exuding love, honor and respect for the people you serve, they will in turn love, honor and respect you. "The measure you measure with, will be measured back to you." If you love, honor and respect them, they will give the same back to you, "pressed down, shaken together, will they pour it into your lap."

Catholics still want to love and respect their priests. It is the individual priest's gift to lose.

## DISCUSSION STARTERS

1. Most dioceses try to place newly ordained priests in pastoral assignments that promise a successful match. How will you handle an assignment that feels like a mismatch for you?

2. What are some of the things you would say to your new parish community on your first Sunday?

3. What are some of the ways you could get to know your parishioners?

4. When is it appropriate for you to leave the fraternal corrections to the pastor and when is it appropriate for you, as an associate pastor, to handle?

5. What are some of the appropriate things that you can ask parishioners to do for you? What are some inappropriate things you could ask parishioners to do for you?

# LACK OF IMAGINATION, FORM WARS, DOWNWARD SPIRALING TALK

*Without a vision, the people perish.*
Proverbs 29:18

Three of the most powerful negative forces that every new priest will have to confront as a leader in our Church are what I call: lack of imagination, form wars and downward spiraling talk.

## LACK OF IMAGINATION

The first thing that is holding us back as a Church is our lack of imagination. I am convinced that imagination is the biggest shortage in the Roman Catholic Church today. Yes, we are in labor, giving birth to a renewed Church, but some would have us believe that these labor pains are really death rattles. What we need is certainly not another round of nervous hand-wringing and blame, but people who are willing to make imaginative new connections. Jesus was right on target when he said that the worldly are a lot more enterprising in dealing with their own kind than we are! We have more resources, more personnel and more technology available to us than our ancestors in the faith ever dreamed about. We just haven't figured out an effective way to marshal them in the service of the gospel.

Every diocese in this country has seen the rise of huge, independent Christian Churches. A large amount of their rapid growth is coming from a huge influx of former Roman Catholics. When I am asked about this phenomenon, my answer is always the same: This is not about their strength; this is about our weakness. Compared to the money, resources and technology that our fathers and mothers in the faith had when they built our great institutions, we are knee-deep in opportunities, but we cannot get our act together to save our lives. The hard truth of the matter is, we are losing members, especially Hispanic members, and it is our fault.

The thing that all of my assignments had in common was this: I was warned before every one of them that the situation I was going into was hopeless and that nothing could be done.

If I had been Bishop Flaget coming down the Ohio, reaching Louisville in 1811 "with not a cent in my purse," faced with a frontier diocese two or three times larger than France, knowing little English and with nine priests for nine and a half states, I would have looked at the situation, turned around and gone back to France, saying it was hopeless and nothing could be done.

By the grace of God, I refused to listen to all the naysayers, tried my best to be imaginative and lived to see some incredible things happen in every one of my assignments, especially at our cathedral, where we saw the congregation grow from 100 households to more than 1600 households, the parish budget go from $90,000 to $900,000, from a ratty old complex to a $20,000,000 restoration and expansion project – an expansion that continues to this day.

Many years ago, I was given an eye-opening insight into our lack of imagination. I was watching television one evening. It was a show about people who had been injured in one way or another. Some were victims of disease, and some were victims of accidents. There was a young man in a wheel chair with one of his legs amputated. He was handsome with an athletic build. He talked a lot about how the accident had changed his life. He was so angry about the unfairness of his situation. He was severely depressed about the loss of what used to be.

It got to be too much to listen to so I turned the channel for relief. There on the screen, in a close-up shot, was another handsome young man with an athletic build and a broad grin. This young man was coming down the mountain on skis, snow flying everywhere. It wasn't until he got to the bottom of the hill that I noticed his legs. He turned out to be a one-legged skier competing in the Handicapped Olympics!

I suddenly had one of those insights that strike like lightning. Something clicked in my head that day. I suddenly realized that I had been both of those young men at one time or another in my life. It made me realize once again that life is always asking us to choose which one we want to be. What is the difference between these two young men? It is a different attitude toward the same problem. One gave up and the other got up! As Henry Ford put it, "Those who think they can and those who think they can't are both right."

Often, what happens to us is not as important as how we respond to what happens to us. The same is true of the Church. Many of our once vigorous old institutions have given up. Institutions, of course, don't give up; people do, one at a time! The people who belong to these institutions have fallen into the habit of sitting in their rocking chairs reminiscing about the good old days and being angry that things are going from bad to worse. They talk in tones of "poor me." They deliver their "we don't have this and we don't have that" speeches to anyone who will listen. They engage in nursing home talk about glorious pasts and grim futures. Having quit dreaming, all they hope for is survival.

There are a rare few religious institutions, however, who have decided to get up, not seeking to recover the good old days, but rather to create some new good old days. They set out to create a second or third golden age. They deal with what is rather than what used to be or what ought to be. They deal with the reality of their situations and turn their minds to creativity. They get out of the back seat and get behind the wheel. They stop being victims and learn to ski again in spite of a missing leg or two!

I first experienced the need for imagination as a newly ordained priest when I was sent to the home missions. I was sent into that situation without one day's training in evangelism, how to start a parish or how to understand Bible Belt culture. When I looked around for help, I realized there was nothing readily available in the Catholic Church, nor was there money available at that time to take advantage of it, even if it did exist! I finally turned to our Protestant friends at McCormick Presbyterian Seminary in Chicago. They brought their teachers to us on a regional basis. Three and a half years later, I graduated with a Doctor of Ministry degree in the area of parish revitalization, and they paid for it! I got a full scholarship on two grounds: minority religion and poverty income!

With so many parishes in need of revitalization, where are the imaginative programs in our own Church to stem this tide? We needed them several years ago! Many dioceses have binders on how to close parishes, but not even a pamphlet on how to keep them open. As a Church, we are getting very good at pulling the plug on gasping parishes, and we keep creating more gasping parishes to unplug.

## FORM WARS

The second thing that is killing us is what I will call our form wars, characterized by brash assaults on old religious forms by so-called liberals and the idolatrous worship of old religious forms by so-called conservatives. As far as I am concerned, they are both wrong. With honest and compassionate dialogue, we have the potential to save the best of the old and open ourselves to the best of the new. So much energy is wasted, so much good will lost, in this war that hurts everyone.

While this elitist war rages on, our people are crossing parish boundaries, diocesan boundaries and even denominational boundaries looking for real spiritual food, looking for alternatives to the unsatisfactory experiences they find in their parishes. This doesn't even mention the glaring fact that many of our expensive Catholic school students don't even attend Eucharist on Sundays and quit the Church altogether immediately after graduation.

Religion has two sides: the *exoteric* and the *esoteric*. The exoteric aspect of religion is concerned with the forms of religion, with correct adherence to the rituals, officially approved practices and precepts of a particular faith tradition. The focus of

64

the esoteric is concerned with the essence of religion, with those things that guide people to a more intimate relationship with God.

Recent Catholicism, I believe, is still overly exoteric in its focus. While we fight over what forms to keep and what forms to invent, we are losing contact with our own spiritual growth tradition. We are failing to distinguish the medium from the message. Both liberals and conservatives are more focused on the medium than the message, putting *how* we do things ahead of *why* we do things. Both liberals and conservatives are still too focused on informing, conforming and reforming: assenting to certain facts, following certain rules and correcting certain behaviors. As important as all these are, they are not of the essence. As Kenneth Woodward wrote in *Commonweal* back in 1994, "I have done my share of institutional criticism ... But what offends me most is the romantic notion that all the ills of the Church reside within the institution – so that if we could reform it, we ourselves would be better Christians. The truth quite often is the other way around."

In this new millennium, let us seek to renew the Church, not primarily by manipulating structures, but through graced personal conversion and courageous transformation, one heart at a time. Jesus did not call for the transformation of structures, but the conversion of hearts. He knew that only converted hearts will know what forms to change and what forms to preserve.

Karl Rahner's prediction is coming true. "The devout Christian of the future will either be a 'mystic,' one who has 'experienced' something, or he will cease to be anything at all." For many Catholics today, there has been no movement of the heart, just more arguments between the left and the right on how to arrange the deck chairs on the Titanic. With a rapacious appetite for spiritual growth that organized religion is failing to feed, people are turning to the thin soup of the new age movement. Some people still don't get it. The sterility of organized religion gave birth to the new age movement.

# DOWNWARD SPIRALING TALK

The third thing that is killing us is our downward spiraling talk. *The Art of Possibility* makes this observation: "Every industry or profession has its own version of downward spiraling talk, as does every relationship. Focusing on the abstraction of scarcity, downward spiraling talk creates an unassailable story about the limits to what is possible and tells us compellingly how things are going from bad to worse. The more attention you shine on a particular subject, the more evidence of it will grow. Attention is like light and air and water. Shine attention on obstacles and problems, and they multiply lavishly."[9] Whether it is a priest shortage, financial shortage or parish closings, the problems multiply lavishly through self-fulfilling prophecies, through constant downward spiraling talk. Again, Henry Ford is right: "Those who think they can and those who think they can't are both right."

Look at our spiritual ancestors, those who built our great parishes and institutions. They had little money, but they had faith, they had determination, they were creative, and they had a vision and a can-do spirit. In contrast, many of our leaders, having quit dreaming and calling us to greatness, seem satisfied with maintenance and keeping order, rather than articulating a vision and marshalling the troops. In the absence of a vision, with its upward spiraling talk, we are each driven by our own agendas: finding people whose interests match ours and being inattentive to those with whom we appear to have little in common. We sink into tribalism. In a Church without vision, it's every dog for himself.

A vision attracts money and personnel, be they clergy or lay. Catholics give 1.1% of their income to the Church, compared to Protestants, who give 2.2%. I believe that is because they are not given a vision, not challenged to greatness; because they are bored, not because they have fewer resources. As Carl Sandburg wrote, "Nothing happens without first a vision." If we were Protestants, we would double our income for new programs overnight!

We can, if we think we can! We can thrive and grow as a Church if we dare make imaginative new connections. It might shock you to know that approximately 65% of the $20,000,000 renovation and expansion of our cathedral facilities and programs came from non-Catholics! (When the first Catholic parish in Louisville was built, the mother parish of our cathedral parish, 90% of the funds came from Protestants.) The revitalization and restoration of our cathedral was made possible through imaginative new connections, by creating a new vision for an old cathedral. The downward spiraling talkers said that revitalizing a center city parish could not be done, that such places only have one golden age. Thank God we upward spiraling talkers did not listen to them!

## CONCLUSION

Our losses to the new mega-churches are about our weakness, not their strength. Creativity has rarely been encouraged in organized religion. Even when Churches find themselves in a desert of ineffectiveness, they tend to defend the merits of the desert rather than find a way out. Pope John XXIII was a notable exception. He realized, in the words of Thomas Merton, that "tradition is creative, always original, always opening out to new directions for an old journey."

When Pope John XXIII opened the Second Vatican Council he spoke these words: "The substance of … faith is one thing, and the way in which it is presented is another. We shall take pains to present to the people of this age God's truth in its integrity and purity that they may understand it and gladly assent to it. The Church considers that she meets the needs of the present day by demonstrating the validity of her teaching rather than condemnations."[10]

Since it takes imagination to "demonstrate the validity of her teaching" so that "people may understand it and gladly assent to it," the restorationists would have us return to force and severity. Like our spiritual ancestors, the Israelites, many cowards with little faith and nerve have turned back at the very sight of a desert.

Maybe we were naïve when we set out on this journey toward a new Church. Maybe we have worshiped a few golden calves along the way, and maybe some have dropped out along the way because the going got rough, but we must keep the dream alive and press on. We must "demonstrate the validity of our message so that people today can understand it and gladly assent to it." To do that we must not only look back, but also look forward and make imaginative connections between the two. Again, Thomas Merton has the words for us! "Those who are not humble hate their pasts and push them out of sight, just as they cut down the growing and green things that spring up inexhaustibly in the present."

The challenge of our age is to do what Matthew did for his people when he wrote his gospel: weave the new and the old together into a new understanding. To do that we must take a stand against our lack of imagination, our form wars and our downward spiraling talk! There are many good things going on in our parishes, but that does not negate the fact that we are up to our ears in missed opportunities.

## DISCUSSION STARTERS

1. Name some situations in our Church that could use some new imagination. Do you have any imaginative new ideas to address those situations?

2. What did our ancestors, who built our great institutions, have that we do not have today? What do we have that these ancestors did not have? Why do you think there is so little imagination in today's Church?

3. What is the biggest obstacle to having enough priests to serve our parishes today? What can you do as a priest to help overcome that obstacle?

4. Why do you think people today are leaving the Church and turning to such things as the new age movement and independent mega-churches? What can you do as a priest to help people meet their spiritual hunger within the Church?

5. What suggestions do you have to bridge the gap between the liberals and conservatives of our Church?

6. How can you, as a new priest, help stem the tide of negativity and downward spiraling talkin our Church?

# MINISTERIAL BOUNDARIES

*Good fences make good neighbors.*
Robert Frost

I used to think that statement was so cynical, so anti-social. I naïvely thought that it should read, "Good neighbors don't need fences." After thirty-five years of priesthood, I am older and wiser. I have come to appreciate the wisdom of Mr. Frost's poem.

By definition, a boundary is a limit or edge that defines one thing as separate from another. Every living organism is separated from every other living organism by a physical barrier. This limit can be breached by injury or other organisms. If the breach is severe enough or if the invading organism is toxic or hostile, the host organism can die. An intact physical boundary preserves life. The perfect example is your skin. It is a boundary. Everything within your skin is the physical you. Even the parts within you have boundaries, one from another: perforate your colon, pierce your aorta and see how long you live! Breached boundaries can kill. Intact physical boundaries preserve life.

That most of us can agree on, but there are other boundaries that extend beyond the physical. We become aware of this when someone stands too close. It is as if we are surrounded by an invisible circle, a comfort zone. This zone is fluid. A lover can stand closer than most friends, and friends can stand closer than a stranger. With someone who is hostile, we might need a great deal of distance.

We have other boundaries as well: emotional, spiritual, sexual and relational. (1) An emotional boundary is a set of feelings and reactions that are distinctly ours because of our history, perceptions, values, concerns and goals. We can find people who react similarly, but no one reacts precisely as we do. (2) Our spiritual boundaries are just as unique. No one can tell us what to believe. We can be assisted, but not forced. Our spiritual development comes from within our inner selves, as Vatican Council II taught us about the role of conscience. Priests, especially, need to remember that "People judge by externals, but only God can see into hearts." (3) We have sexual boundaries, limits on what is safe and appropriate sexual behavior from others. Normally, we have a choice about whom we interact with sexually and the extent of that interaction. (4) We have relational boundaries. The roles we play define the limits of appropriate interaction with others.

Boundaries are important. They bring order into our lives and into our communities. With good boundaries, we can have the wonderful assurance that comes from knowing we can and will protect ourselves, and those entrusted to us, from the ignorance, meanness, thoughtlessness and sins of others. Boundary violations can be conscious and premeditated, but more often than not, they happen quickly and unconsciously. Like any fence, boundaries require maintenance and vigilance. Boundaries are not always rigid. There are age-related boundaries, cultural-related boundaries and even time-related boundaries. What is appropriate for one age group or one culture may not be appropriate for others. Spilling your guts about the details of your sexual history to a counselor or confessor may be appropriate, while doing it from the pulpit probably will not be!

Relationships are at the heart of pastoral ministry.[11] Priests and religious, with their highly complex roles and involvements, can easily become entangled in boundary violations. Problems arise when priests and religious fail to be aware of their roles as ministers with others. Boundary violations occur when a priest or religious implicitly or explicitly defines a relationship inaccurately.

Ministerial boundaries are the limits that allow for a safe connection in a ministerial relationship based on the other person's need. Consequently, a boundary violation occurs when ministers act out of their own needs in the relationship. Boundary violations usually involve a series of interactions rather than a single event. Many violations begin as innocent situations that feel good both to the minister and the other person. Problems arise when a priest or religious attempts to be friends and denies his or her own power and status in representing the Church.

The issue of boundaries is very important today, because so many of the social controls are gone. As a result of this, we need to know ourselves very well, because we often operate from ulterior motives, all the while being in denial of what is really going on. The person in the power position is *always* responsible for inappropriate interactions that occur, regardless of who initiated them. It is the duty of the priest or religious to set boundaries.

When are priests and religious most likely to violate ministerial boundaries? There are specific issues, personal struggles and behavioral patterns commonly shared by those who engage in boundary violations: lack of intimacy, poor social networks, loneliness, isolation, loss, lack of sexual awareness, stress, burnout, inappropriate use of alcohol, or a history of poor emotional boundaries, including possible victimization themselves and a failure to heed the concerns of others about inappropriate behaviors.

"Good fences make good neighbors." Boundaries are freeing and facilitating structures that enable us to relate and minister with comfort and confidence.

## DISCUSSION STARTERS

1. How have you been affected personally by the boundary violations of other priests and religious, especially the boundary violations of those involved in the recent sexual abuse scandal?

2. Why do you think they violated the boundaries they violated?

3. When are you most susceptible to boundary violations? What steps can you take to prevent those violations from happening?

4. What is your responsibility when you witness other priests, religious or staff violating ministerial boundaries?

5. We are more aware of sexual boundary violations than of others. Give some examples of emotional and spiritual boundary violations. What is behind these types of violations?

# THE SPIRITUALITY
# OF A DIOCESAN PRIEST[12]

*Holy Orders and Matrimony are directed toward the salvation*
*of others; if they contribute as well to personal salvation,*
*it is through service to others that they do so.*
Catechism of the Catholic Church 1534

As a seminarian formed by Sulpicians and Benedictines for twelve years, then a diocesan priest for thirty-five years, and finally back in a Benedictine-run seminary as a diocesan-priest staff member, I have the advantage of seeing diocesan priest spirituality from both sides: how it's taught in the seminary and how it's lived in the real world of a diocesan priest. Additionally, as a vocation director for seven years, I can say that the spiritual formation of seminarians today is excellent, but because it is derivative of charisms not necessarily one's own, I can say from experience that it does not always translate well after ordination.

Most writers on the subject of the spirituality of diocesan priests agree on two things: (1) The diocesan priest's spirituality is eclectic, an amalgam of quasi-monastic Jesuit, Dominican and Franciscan spiritualities often filtered through Sulpician and Irish approaches to the spiritual life, and (2) The diocesan priest continues to search for a spirituality properly his own.

The spirituality of the diocesan priest is, of course, rooted first of all in the spirituality of a baptized person, the daily living out of the death and resurrection of Christ. Like the early disciples of Jesus, a priest must make a fundamental decision for radical faith in Jesus. He must be willing to risk it all, and to bet his life, on Jesus. He must constantly nurture a personal relationship with Jesus and model his heart on the inclusive heart of Jesus, for whom the reign of God was open to all. Acting *in persona Christi*, he must love without limit and offer mercy without measure. This living and obvious faith gives authenticity, vibrancy, meaning and efficacy to his role as *pastor* of the flock.

This baptismal spirituality is lived out in the specific context of his ministry as a priest, just as married people live out a spirituality in the specific context of being a marriage partner and parent. The Catechism says that these two sacraments are geared not merely to personal salvation, but toward the salvation of others. "...if they contribute as well to personal salvation, it is through service to others that they do so" (#1534). The spirituality of both a marriage partner and a diocesan priest comes out of the context of living their specific calls well.

At its most basic level, presbyteral spirituality is ecclesial; it is *for* the Church. The diocesan priest is called from the laity to live among the laity, to serve the mission and ministry of the laity. Here the diocesan priest has three functions: preacher of the Word, presider at the celebration of the sacraments and leader of faith communities. The specific context of a diocesan priest's spirituality, then, is wrapped up in doing these three things well, just as a married person's spirituality is wrapped up in being a good spouse and a good parent.

There are two important Greek words for good, *agathos* and *kalos*. *Agathos* means good as in morally good. *Kalos* means good as in effective or good at something. Pope John Paul II, then, could be said to be *agathos* and *kalos*, a good person who is good at shepherding. I would say that an emerging spirituality of the diocesan priest should involve being a good person *and* being good at priesting. An emerging spirituality of the diocesan priest will be a matter of both, not of one or the other.

In the pre-Vatican II spirituality of diocesan priests, seminary training emphasized *agathos*. It focused primarily on the ascetical and devotional aspects of the inner life. Celebrating the Eucharist, praying the breviary, saying the rosary and adopting other devotional practices were the source and fuel of his spirituality. Since Vatican Council II, we have seen a shift of emphasis that has added the *kalos*. This shift is more developmental than disjunctive, for it builds on the traditional staples

76

of priestly spirituality. Priestly spirituality has evolved into an interdependence of *agathos* (a personal-based spirituality) and *kalos* (a ministry-based spirituality).

The emerging spirituality of the diocesan priest, therefore, may be thought of as a dialectical spirituality that is rooted in his life of faith and prayer and, at the same time, shaped and forged by the exercise of his ministerial priesthood. The former pole of the dialectic, personal holiness, is common to all the baptized. It is through the latter pole of the dialectic that we discover those things that allow us to speak of a spirituality proper to a diocesan priest. The spirituality unique to the diocesan priest is forged and shaped in his threefold role in the faith community: preacher, presider and leader, not merely in personal ascetical and devotional practices.

If a diocesan priest's spirituality is *ecclesial*, not merely *personal*, the priest is regarded as one who serves a *people-centered* Church, a very different emphasis from that of a pre-Vatican II *priest-centered* Church. In a Church understood as the people of God, the priest functions as a servant of God's people and as one whose ministry is exercised in cooperation with and is interdependent upon other diverse ministries in the Church. The spirituality of the diocesan priest, then, will be forged and shaped in his threefold role in the faith community as preacher of the Word, presider at the celebration of the Sacraments and coordinator of charisms. It is not enough for a diocesan priest to simply be *holy*; he must also be *good at* his three basic ministries.

I will spend a little time talking about the homily-based and presider-based parts of a diocesan priest's spirituality, but I will spend more time on the servant-leader based spirituality of diocesan priests. Here is one important note. Even though studies reveal that most priests enjoy the second of the three functions of priesthood, presider at the celebration of the sacraments, and some today would favor being "cultic" priests, we cannot be "cafeteria" priests, picking one and neglecting the other. We are called to do all three at the same time.

# THE HOMILY-BASED SPIRITUALITY OF THE DIOCESAN PRIEST

*"When I found your words, I devoured them; they became my joy and the happiness of my heart." –* Jeremiah 15:16

> The People of God finds its unity first of all through the Word of the living God, which is quite properly sought from the lips of priests. Since no one can be saved who has not first believed, priests, as co-workers with their bishops, have as their primary duty the proclamation of gospel of God to all.[13]

Besides saying that preaching is the "primary duty" of priests, the council encouraged priests to preach at weekday Eucharist as well as Sunday Eucharist and the celebration of the other sacraments. This call to daily preaching, rather than being just another one of the things a priest does, is at the heart of a diocesan priest's spirituality. Preaching well, this often, requires daily wallowing in the Word. Struggling to understand it so that its power to transform can be experienced and communicated becomes the centerpiece of his spiritual growth as a diocesan priest.

If the primary duty of priests is to preach, then it's easier said than done! Even though Vatican Council II made this decree in 1965, ask any number of honest Catholics 40 years later and they will tell you that priests are still failing in their primary duty. Catholics are crossing parish and diocesan boundaries looking for solid spiritual food, and when they fail to find it, they leave us to join those independent mega-churches that are springing up all over the country and sucking people out of our parishes at an alarming rate. It's past time to translate "the primary duty of the priest is to preach" from wishful thinking to an obvious reality! In this chapter, I would like to outline several things that I believe will help produce preaching specialists for the Church.

# THE PURPOSE OF PREACHING

The purpose of preaching is "…to summon all men urgently to conversion and to holiness."[14] You cannot summon others to conversion and holiness without having been converted to holiness yourself. Otherwise you may become another kind of preaching specialist, a clever manipulator of people for your own ends, but you will not be a priest, a medium of God's good news. You may be able to entertain, make people laugh or cry or give you their money, but you will never be able to lead them to conversion and to holiness. "Faith comes through hearing, and what is heard is the Word of Christ!" (Romans 10:17)

The preacher's first test is his ability to call people to discipleship. The preacher's final test is his ability to become the disciple he calls others to be, to practice what he preaches, to put up or shut up.

# PREACH WHAT?

We are called "not to preach our own wisdom, but God's Word."[15] We are called to preach the gospel. The word gospel means good news. Can you tell me in a few words what the good news is that Jesus came to bring to the world and you are commissioned to announce? I cannot believe that there are priests and deacons who have been preaching for years, seminarians about to be ordained after five or six years in the seminary, who cannot answer that question.

The good news is, and the bottom line of every homily should be, this: God loves us without condition, no ifs, ands or buts about it! It's the message of the Covenant. It's the message of the parables. It's the message of the Passion, Death and Resurrection of Jesus. The biggest problem behind most preaching occurs when the preacher himself does not understand or believe this good news, and he ends up preaching an opposing message of conditional love.

We are called to preach the gospel, not our opinions, prejudices, pet peeves or our own wisdom. If our trips to Europe don't help enlighten the gospel text, then don't bring them up! Besides, it is insensitive at best not to think about all those families in front of us who will never be able to afford such trips. I don't care how funny our latest jokes are – if they don't enlighten what Jesus had to say, we need to save them for another occasion! We are not called to do stand-up comedy from the pulpit. Preaching is not a scripture class or a theology lecture. People are not interested in where we went on vacation, how funny we are, what we are mad about or what we know. Preaching is not about us. It's about helping people respond to Christ's invitation to discipleship. We are the earthenware jar, not the treasure!

"… all preaching of the Church must be nourished and ruled by sacred Scripture. For in the sacred books, the Father who is in heaven meets His children with great love and speaks with them; and the force and power in the word of God is so great that it remains the support and energy of the Church, the strength and faith of her sons (and daughters), the food of the soul, the pure and perennial source of spiritual life."[16] "In pastoral care, appropriate use must be made not only of theological principles, but also of the findings of the secular sciences, especially psychology and sociology. Thus the faithful can be brought to live the faith in a more thorough and mature way."[17]

"The priest is to be a bridge builder who links the human and the divine. To do so effectively, he must know the terrain on both ends of the bridge" (Fr. Robert Schwartz). The bridge must know himself as well. One of the most infamous examples of the preacher not knowing himself is the preacher who has not dealt with his own sexuality, who has not integrated his own sexual energy. He will be a preacher obsessed, not with the good news, but with sex, sexual morality and other people's sex lives, as a substitute for dealing with his own sexual issues. This will be done, of course, under the cover of defending morality.

# A PASSION FOR PREACHING

*"I say to myself, I will not mention him. I will speak his name no more. But then it becomes like a fire burning in my heart, imprisoned in my bones; I grow weary holding it in, I cannot endure it."* – Jeremiah 20:9

"The priest is able to proclaim the word of God only to the extent that that word has burned into his heart and is lived in his life."[18] Before you can be a Samuel, "not permitting any word of his to be without effect" (I Samuel 3:19), you must be a Jeremiah for whom preaching became "like a fire burning in my heart, imprisoned in my bones; I grow weary holding it in" (Jeremiah 20:9) and "When I found your words, I devoured them; they became my joy and the happiness of my heart" (Jeremiah 15:16). "For a man's words flow out of what fills his heart" (Luke 6:45). *"Nemo dat quod non habet,"* or "If you don't have it, you can't give it!" (Old Latin Maxim). "If the story is in you, it has to come out" (William Faulkner).

Serious preaching is not for the spiritually lazy. Only those who are on serious, personal, spiritual quests can ever become effective preaching specialists. The preaching specialist must know the word of God, know people and know himself. A preaching specialist's main tools are the Scriptures, the newspaper and personal reflection on his own personal and spiritual experience.

# FOCUSED ATTENTION

No one is born a preaching specialist. It starts with a dream. It is nourished by faith. It is perfected by focused attention. Anything you pay attention to, you can get better at! If you really believe that you can be a preaching specialist, you will see it, but it doesn't come cheap. It takes years of focused attention. Translating a dream into reality takes great courage. Doubt is a constant enemy. When doubt reigns, there is a strong temptation to let go of part of the dream as a way of resolving inevitable tensions. Success depends on the ability to remain enthusiastic, focused and purposeful to the end.

I am a living example of focused attention. I was so bashful that I could barely read in front of my classmates when I was in the seminary. After ordination, I found myself in a home mission situation where a preaching specialist was needed. I decided that I could be such a preaching specialist and set out to rise to the occasion. I decided to be what I imagined. With hard work and focused attention, I have been a preaching specialist for 35 years now. I have given thousands of homilies and hundreds of retreats, parish missions and days of recollection. I have published three collections of homilies, produced six taped collections of homilies, write a column of popular spirituality each week for our diocesan paper and even teach homiletics now and then.

Want it and you can have it! Believe it and you will see it! As an old proverb says, "When the student is ready, the teacher will appear!" "God loves to help him who strives to help himself" (Aeschylus, Fragment 223).

## ORGANIZED FOR SUCCESS

Homiletics training has greatly improved in our seminaries in the last several years. There is very little attention paid, however, to the practical steps necessary to produce several homilies each week while doing all the things one is called on to do. The dream of being a homiletics specialist needs to have an implementation plan.

Every would-be preaching specialist, I believe, must develop his own personal homiletics resource center. This well-organized center should have a comfortable place to think and work, a computer program for the storing and retrieval of his work, a library of commentaries, familiar quotations, a biblical thesaurus, a regular thesaurus, a paper filing system for clippings and ideas, a hand-held tape recorder with blank tapes, and a journal of personal experiences.

In my own personal homiletics resource center, I even have a music system and exercise equipment. I have found that my mind seems to open up between sets on the exercise equipment and the computer, especially in the presence of soothing music. Whoever thought about putting gym time and homiletics time together? This is a unique example of the "working smarter, not just harder" plan that all priests today must create for themselves in the fast-paced world of parish ministry.

Finally, I ask people for feedback. I have several boxes of letters from people who have sent in their affirmations, ideas, constructive criticisms. I have found that when I try hard to feed them, they in turn feed me, setting up a cycle of energy that gives me the courage and determination to keep preaching. Their responses have made it all worthwhile. There is something magical in helping people get in touch with God.

# CONCLUSION

Roman Catholics are starving for good preaching. They are moving from parish to parish looking for it. When they don't find it within our Church, they feel free to leave and look for it in other places. "And how can they believe unless they have heard of him? And how can they hear unless there is someone to preach?" (Romans 10:14) If you are not part of the solution, you will be part of the problem. Become a preaching specialist! Let preaching be *the* major component of your spirituality as a diocesan priest.

## The Presider-Based Spirituality of the Diocesan Priest

Preaching Scripture and celebrating Sacraments are one and the same: proclamations of Good News. Both are invitations seeking a response. In the Vatican II Church, at long last, we can do both together.

The sacraments, privileged moments in communicating the divine life to humankind, are at the very core of priestly ministry. When priests preside at the celebration of the sacraments, they act *in persona Christi*.

As such, two things are required:

1. Even though Christ can act through flawed human beings, if one is to act in persona Christi, a credible lifestyle is a must. St. Augustine says, "Christ's gift is not profaned by a weak minister; what flows through him keeps its purity, and what passes through him remains. What passes through defiled human beings is not itself defiled." Even though the message does not depend on the goodness of the messenger, again Pope John Paul reminds us that "a priest should mold his life in such a way that he becomes a bridge and not an obstacle."

2. A high standard of ceremony and liturgical celebration, free from spectacle and personal taste for styles foreign to the community, is required. The best dictum may be "do what is in the book, with its approved options, well."

The core of priestly ministry is the celebration of the Eucharist, the source and summit of the Christian life. Along with Baptism and Confirmation, the Eucharist is one of the three sacraments of initiation. Reconciliation, along with Anointing, are the sacraments of healing. Holy Orders and Matrimony are sacraments of service.

## The Servant Leader-Based Spirituality of the Diocesan Priest

This may be the hardest dimension of the spirituality of diocesan priests, and it is becoming even harder. Priests are leaders of the community – not the only leaders, but leaders, nonetheless.

Whom do they lead, and where do they lead? Pope John Paul II tells us, "Through the ministerial priesthood, Christ gives to priests in the Spirit a particular gift so that they can help the people of God exercise faithfully and fully the common priesthood which it has received." He also says, "The priesthood is not an institution that exists alongside the laity or 'above' it. The priesthood is 'for' the laity, and precisely for this reason it possesses a ministerial character, that is to say, one 'of service.'" Leading lay people to faithfully and fully exercise their baptismal priesthood is the mission of diocesan priests.

A pastor's spirituality is built around his call to shepherd. The essential object of his action as a pastor is the common good. As such, he must move from his own personal point of view to a viewing point. Unlike a seminarian, a pastor does not have the luxury of living merely in his personal point of view. The difference in being a seminarian with a personal point of view and being a public person as a priest, especially a pastor, cannot be underestimated. Some never understand the difference, dividing congregations along the lines of "those who are with me and those who are against me."

A priest, especially a pastor, can never be the servant of an ideology or of a faction. "The pastor always moves from a personal to a community dimension." "It is their task, therefore, to reconcile differences of mentality in such a way that no one may feel himself a stranger in the community of the faithful. Priests are defenders of the common good, with which they are charged in the name of the bishop. At the same time, they are strenuous defenders of the truth, lest the faithful be tossed about by every wind of opinion."[19]

Two extremes must be avoided: authoritarianism (exercising his ministry in an overbearing manner) and abdication (disdaining his rightful role of leader). The key word here is *proper* authority.

More than a few veteran observers of the Church insist that the most pressing need facing Catholicism today is the quality of its priestly leadership, the third of the three roles of a priest. No matter how one ranks the quality of priestly leadership on any scale of Church priorities, it is clearly a matter of concern for the vitality of the Church in whatever age the Church finds itself. Exercising proper leadership is an integral part of the diocesan priest's spirituality.

The authenticity and maturity of the priest's spirituality remains the fundamental issue supporting his preaching, presiding and leading. Pastoral skills can be taught, but they remain techniques unless rooted in, and connected to, the spirituality of the diocesan priest.

In short, the spirituality of a diocesan priest involves integrating who a priest is with what a priest does, being a good person with being good at what a priest does, contributing to his own salvation through his service to others.

St. Gregory Nazianzus speaks of this integration when he writes, "Before purifying others, they must purify themselves; to instruct others they must be instructed; they have to become light in order to illuminate and become close to God in order to sanctify."

St. Charles Borromeo speaks of this integration when he writes, "If teaching and preaching is your job, then study diligently and apply yourself to whatever is necessary for doing the job. Be sure that you first preach by the way you live. If you do not, people will notice that you say one thing, but live otherwise, and your words will bring only cynical laughter and a derisive shake of the head."

# FREED UP FOR FULL-TIME SERVICE

Diocesan priests do not take vows, but they do make two important promises to the bishop: celibacy and obedience. Rather than being negatives, both of these make complete availability for apostolic service possible.

## Celibacy

For many centuries, the Roman Catholic Church has required that all its ordained ministers, with the exception of permanent deacons, live a celibate life-style. This long tradition, reaffirmed by Vatican II and subsequently by Popes Paul VI and John Paul II, is the result of many centuries of reflection about the style of life appropriate to ordained ministry.

The celibate commitment has remained the most radical and comprehensive translation of Jesus' call to give up everything for the sake of the kingdom. It takes a highly evolved spiritual person to freely and consciously embrace celibacy and do it justice. This heroic life-style presumes a healthy and well-adjusted person. For that person, celibacy frees him up for a greater good, for full-time service of God's people.

## Obedience

Like celibacy, obedience frees a diocesan priest up for complete availability to perform apostolic service. The promise of obedience is made to the bishop, but it has implications beyond the person of the bishop. It includes a promise to fellow members of the presbyterate. It is a promise to the bishop and fellow priests to be a team player for the sake of their common mission to the People of God.

## DISCUSSION STARTERS

1.  How will the spirituality you have developed as a seminarian change when you become a diocesan priest?

2.  What plans do you have for replacing your seminary spiritual director?

3.  What can you do to make your threefold mission of preacher, presider and leader become the basis of your spirituality as a diocesan priest?

4.  In light of a very busy schedule as a diocesan priest, how do you plan on keeping your preaching as your primary task in fact and not just in name?

5.  Of these three roles, with which do you think you will need additional help?

6.  How do your promises of celibacy and obedience free you up for service?

# WHAT SUPPORT IS AVAILABLE TO DIOCESAN PRIESTS?

*Beloved, you demonstrate your fidelity by all you do for the brothers, even though they are strangers: indeed they have testified to your love before the Church. And you will do a good thing if you continue to help them to continue their journey... We owe it to such men to support them and thus to have a share in the work of truth.*
III John 1:5-8

While each priest is ultimately responsible for his own happiness, diocesan priests have at their disposal a generous array of personal and professional support. Below is a summary of possible personal and professional support available to diocesan priests. Gleaned from various Church documents on priesthood, they will vary from diocese to diocese, but the fundamentals will remain the same.

## Laity

Without priests, the Church would not be able to carry out all those things that are at the very heart of her mission. The priesthood, then, is a gift to the Church as a whole, a benefit to her life and mission. The Church, therefore, is called to safeguard this gift, to esteem it and to love it. The laity, for their part, should realize their obligations toward their priests, and with love they should follow them as shepherds and fathers. They should help their priests by prayer and by sharing their cares so that priests can more readily overcome difficulties and be able to fulfill their duties effectively.

## The Bishop

The bishop should always extend a special love and concern for his priests since they assume, in part, the bishop's own duties and cares and carry the weight of them day by day. He should be concerned about his priests' spiritual, intellectual and material condition, so that they can live holy lives and fulfill their ministry faithfully and effectively. Special attention should be paid to those who are in any sort of danger or who have failed in some respect.

## Fellow Priests

By virtue of their common sacred ordination and mission, all priests are bound together in an ultimate brotherhood. Each and every priest, therefore, is joined to his brother priests by a bond of love, prayer and every kind of cooperation. Older priests should receive younger priests as true brothers and give them a hand with their first assignments in ministry. Young priests should respect the age and experience of their seniors. Priests should be especially solicitous toward other priests who are sick, afflicted, overburdened with work, lonely, away from their homeland or who have failed in some way. Priests should be encouraged to develop some kind of communal life, a shared roof where this is feasible, a common table, or at least frequent and regular gatherings.

## Family and Friends

Celibacy does not preclude warm friendships and intimate relationships. Priests need and value the friendship of laymen and laywomen, Catholic and non-Catholic. Married couples and their families play a key role in the lives of many priests. Families – parents, aunts, uncles, brothers, sisters, nieces, nephews and cousins – form an important support system for priests throughout their priesthood. Priests are encouraged to visit their families, spend holidays with them and stay involved in their lives.

## Financial Compensation

A diocesan priest does not take a vow of poverty, but receives a salary and benefits so that he can live modestly, buy and maintain a car, take a vacation, give to charities and save for his retirement. The diocesan priests within a particular diocese normally receive the same salary, depending on years of ordination, whether they serve in a small mission church, a large suburban parish or an agency of the diocese.

Besides a salary, a priest receives room and board, an annual retreat fee and an annual continuing education fee.

Along with a salary, each parish or agency pays into a retirement plan for the priests who serve them. Since diocesan priests are expected to plan for their own retirement needs, this retirement fund is part of that planning.

# Office of Clergy Personnel

The Office of Clergy Personnel exists to assist the bishop in the appointment of priests to parishes, offices, institutions and other diocesan ministries, as well as provide a process in which the individual priest is part of the decision.

# Office for the Continuing Formation of the Clergy

The Continuing Formation of the Clergy Office exists to give priests a variety of opportunities to learn more about themselves, learn new pastoral skills and deepen their insights into ministry. Each year a variety of workshops, conventions, printed materials and classes are advertised, sponsored or recommended. Each priest receives a generous stipend each year to help him accept responsibility for his continued growth as a person and as a minister.

# Clergy Health Panel

The Clergy Health Panel is there to assist priests who are in need of help with chemical dependency and other addictions.

# Priests' Council

The Priests' Council is a group of priests elected by their fellow priests to represent their concerns in a forum of full and free discussion of the issues pertaining to their pastoral work. This representative group assists the bishop by offering counsel about the pastoral work of the archdiocese from its pool of experience and wisdom. Discussion takes place in regional groups and peer groups. Each regional and peer group sends representatives to the Priests' Council, as well as members elected at large and from religious communities of men. There is a national group of priests who come from Priests' Councils all over the country and meet in an annual convention to share their wisdom and work on common issues.

# Vicar for Clergy

The Vicar for Clergy, a priest of the diocese, acts as the bishop's personal representative to the retired priests of the diocese. This priest helps retired priests deal with their medical, housing, ministry and social needs.

# Retirement Home

A retirement home is usually available to those retired priests who wish to live in close proximity with other retired priests. Diocesan priests, however, are free to work out their own retirement living in any way they choose.

# Presbyteral Assembly

Each year, all the priests of most dioceses hold a week-long Presbyteral Assembly with their bishop. This week is a combination of relaxation, prayer, team building, celebration, discussions, education and renewal. Various priests from within the diocese are asked to share their wisdom, as are priests, religious and lay people from outside the diocese.

## Support Groups

Support Groups are encouraged. Groups of priests freely choose to band together for mutual support in various areas of the diocese. These groups might gather together on their day off for recreation, or they might gather monthly for mutual support. They may be prayer groups, or they may be one of the 12-step groups.

## Annual Retreats and Prayer Days

Annual retreats and prayer days are encouraged. Annual retreats can be done as a group or individually. A variety of opportunities are offered or advertised, but a priest may choose to design his own. A stipend for an annual retreat is part of the priest's compensation package. Various kinds of prayer days are offered several times a year.

## Sabbaticals

Sabbaticals are encouraged. This is an extended time off for renewal, education and growth. A sabbatical can last three to six months. Once a sabbatical plan is approved, the diocese normally pays for many of the expenses involved.

## Spiritual Directors

Every priest is encouraged to find a trusted priest to be his spiritual director. This priest may be one of his fellow diocesan priests, one of the religious priests, a priest in a neighboring diocese or a priest from one of the local monasteries. Some priests choose lay people or members of a religious community to be their spiritual directors.

## Alternative Housing

Most priests live in a rectory provided by the parish they serve or in an apartment or house supplied by the institution in which they minister. Although not universal, some dioceses allow for alternative housing, such as owning one's own home or renting one's own apartment, assuming approval by the bishop and under certain circumstances and restrictions.

# Vacation

Every priest is entitled to and encouraged to take an annual vacation, often up to four weeks a year depending on years of service. The priest is expected to pay for his own vacation out of his salary.

---

## DISCUSSION STARTERS

1. Describe your plans for minding your call after ordination.

2. Pope John Paul II has said that the initial formation of the seminary must be followed by ongoing formation. Are you committed to seeking the continuing formation you will need, especially as you move into being a pastor? If so, what do you plan to do to get that additional education?

3. Are you committed to being personally responsible for your own happiness as a priest? What can you do to make yourself happy and effective as a priest, regardless of circumstances?

4. What ongoing formation programs within your diocese, at your former seminary and around the country do you plan to be involved in?

5. In the above list, which ones will you use most? Which ones do not appeal to you or will probably not be available to you?

---

# REMEMBERING WHY WE DO WHAT WE DO

*Peter got out of the boat and began to walk on the water
toward Jesus. But when he saw how strong the wind was he
became frightened; and beginning to sink, he cried out,
"Lord, save me!" Immediately Jesus stretched
out his hand and caught him.*
Matthew 14:29,30

The life of a diocesan priest today is intense and complicated. It is easy to get lost. It is common to get overwhelmed and forget why we do what we do. When we take our eyes off the prize, we begin to make the essentials accidental and the accidentals essential. If the shepherd is distracted, the sheep are vulnerable. "If the trumpeter is hesitant, who will get ready for battle?" (I Corinthians 14:8) If a priest loses his way, forgets what is really important, begins sweating the small stuff, then he and the people he is called to serve and lead are at risk.

It's hard to be a wounded healer, one who tends to his own wounds while attending the wounds of others. Loneliness, isolation and disillusionment are some of the main reasons cited by those who leave the priesthood within the first five years. If a priest is bleeding emotionally and spiritually, he will have little time or focus to deal with the bleeding of others. At these times, in particular, it is so easy for him to forget why he does what he does.

The expectation placed on priests are many, and often, they are unreal. Trying to measure up is a strain. It's hard for a priest to be good and be good at what he does, to do personal maintenance and task maintenance. Personal maintenance is about keeping one's personal and spiritual house in order. Task maintenance is about keeping one's pastoral skills fine-tuned. At these times, it is easy to get discouraged with oneself. There are so many needs and so little time and energy. When a priest is discouraged, it is easy for him to forget why he does what he does.

Priests not only have to live with their own weakness, but are also affected by the weakness of other priests. Father Bob Silva, in his December 19, 2004, National Federation of Priests' Councils newsletter column, makes these sad remarks: "All is not well with the priesthood in this country. Daily I review the reports telling of priests who have abused children, of those removed from ministry for inappropriate sexual behavior with adults, of priests who have stolen money from their parishes, of priests abusing their authority, of priests who are mean-spirited … Because of some priests' weaknesses and crimes, all priests are weakened and suffer loss of pastoral effectiveness."

Being serious about personal maintenance (watching your weight, getting exercise, taking time off, maintaining friends, being connected to your family, following a prayer life and living a celibate lifestyle) can be overwhelming in what is asked. When a priest is overwhelmed, it is easy for him to forget why he does what he does.

As a priest, being serious about task maintenance, balancing the three essential tasks of priesthood, is so important for the life of the faith community. Preaching is a priest's primary responsibility. Being a finely tuned instrument through which God communicates with his people is an awesome responsibility. Presiding at the celebration of the sacraments is also a serious position in the Church because good liturgy builds faith, while bad liturgy destroys it. Being a leader of a faith community, but not the only leader, is delicate balancing act of great importance, especially when it is done in a factious community.

The details required for doing all this well can be all-consuming. There are Canon Law, liturgical norms and diocesan guidelines to follow. There is the refereeing of fights between warring ecclesiologies, important financial matters to attend to, staff members to be hired and salaries to be negotiated. There are youth groups to drop in on, hospitals to visit, ribbons to cut and mail to answer. It is easy to be inundated and lose perspective. As important as all those things are, they are not of the essence. When the accidentals become essential and the essentials are lost sight of, it is easy for a priest to forget why he does what he does.

What is essential is the good news of God's unconditional love. This unconditional love was revealed at Sinai, but even more elaborately revealed in the person of Jesus. Jesus symbolizes the length and the breadth, the height and depth of God's love. The parables of Jesus describe, even more elaborately than Sinai, the incredible good news that we are loved, without condition. This is the bottom line. This is why we do what we do as priests. If we forget that we are bearers of good news, we have indeed lost our way.

I chose the story of Peter's walk on water as the gospel for my 25th anniversary celebration as a priest because it described my experience as a priest during those first 25 years and because it offered me a pattern to follow in my remaining years as a priest. Looking back, I have somehow been able, to my own surprise, to do things I never thought possible as long as I have kept my eyes fixed on Jesus. It has only been those times when I took my eyes off him and started to focus on how deep the water was and how high the winds that I began to sink. It is so hard, and yet so vitally important, for priests to remember why they do what they do.

Priests act *in persona Christi*. This is the awesome bottom line. This is what every priest must remember and call himself back to, over and over again. If he forgets why he does what he does, all will be lost and his life will make no sense whatsoever. A priest must keep his eyes fixed on Jesus.

## DISCUSSION STARTERS

1. What do you do and how do you act when you are overwhelmed? What do you traditionally do to regain your balance and focus?

2. Loneliness is often cited as the reason newly ordained priests leave in their first five years. How can you prevent loneliness from overtaking you? What strategies have you developed to cope with it?

3. What can you do to regularly remind yourself of why you do what you do as a priest?

4. How have the sexual abuse scandal and other bad behaviors of priests affected you, personally and as a priest-to-be?

5. Do you have any stories or passages from scripture that seem to help you regain your focus when you are overwhelmed?

6. To whom can you turn if you find yourself in a serious vocational crisis?

# MINDING YOUR CALL

*All things that resist change are changed by that resistance*
*in ways undesired and undesirable.*
Garry Wills

If I were a seminarian today, I would be scared, very scared. Fear wouldn't stop me from becoming a priest, but I would resolve to tackle my fear by seizing every opportunity to prepare myself for the reality facing me.

As a seminarian, it is hard to imagine what will be expected of new priests in the next few years. The number of priests is shrinking, but the amount of work is growing. Huge responsibilities are being placed on new priests in less time after ordination.

It is becoming obvious that seminary training alone is no longer enough. Because there are so many things seminaries cannot prepare new priests to handle, and because the period of internship has been shortened or eliminated in some cases, it is becoming obvious that ongoing formation is no longer a luxury, but a necessity.

If I were a seminarian today, I would be so anxious about what I was getting into that I would begin planning my ongoing formation even before I left the seminary, as Pope John Paul II encourages.

To get myself in the frame of mind to do ongoing formation, I would listen to that voice that calls me to strive to be the very best priest I can be, and I would refuse to listen to the one that tells me to do just enough to get by on. I cannot imagine doing priesthood halfheartedly. I cannot imagine being satisfied with being unhappy, bored and ineffective as a priest. I would have to be a priest with passion or not at all.

# FORMATION OF THE INDIVIDUAL PRIEST

Pope John Paul II may have best summarized the need for, and resistance to, ongoing formation when he said, "With priests who have just come out of the seminary, a certain sense of "having had enough" is quite understandable when faced with new times of study and meeting. But the idea that priestly formation ends on the day one leaves the seminary is false and dangerous and needs to be totally rejected."[20]

"We all have a sick self and a healthy self. No matter how neurotic or even psychotic we may be, even if we seem to be totally fearful and completely rigid, there is still part of us, however small, that wants to grow, that likes change and development, that is attracted to the new and the unknown, that is willing to do the work and take the risks involved in spiritual evolution. And no matter how seemingly healthy and spiritually evolved we are, there is still a part of us, however small, that does not want us to exert ourselves, that clings to the old and familiar, fearful of any change or effort, desiring comfort at any cost and absence of pain at any price, even if the penalty be ineffectiveness, stagnation or regression."[21]

Pope John Paul firmly supports the need for post-seminary formation. He says that it is important to be aware of, and respect, the intrinsic link between the formation before ordination and formation after ordination. He calls seminary formation *initial* and formation after seminary *ongoing.* He makes the point that long-term preparation for ongoing formation should take place in the seminary, where encouragement needs to be given to future priests to look forward to it, seeing its necessity, its advantage and the Spirit in which it should be undertaken, and the appropriate conditions for its realization need to be insured.[22]

Pope John Paul II makes the point that this ongoing formation needs to be something better than "seminary warmed-over." He calls for "relatively new content and methods." Saint Meinrad's **Institute for Priests and Presbyterates** is a recent effort to design a program of follow-up for priests in their first five years. It will offer interdiocesan, holistic support for newly ordained priests in the practice of ministry.

This interdiocesan approach is supported by Pope John Paul II when he says, "Often it will be suitable, or indeed necessary, for bishops of neighboring dioceses … to come together and join forces to be able to offer initiatives for permanent formation that are better organized and more interesting …"[23] This **Institute** is a serious effort to heed the words of Pope John Paul II about not breaking that intrinsic link between the initial formation of the seminary and ongoing formation. The aim of ongoing formation is to integrate who a priest is with what he does. The People of God have a right to competent pastoral leadership. Neither holiness nor goodwill alone can replace competence. A priest today must not only be good and mean well, he must also be good at what he does. Ongoing education in the practical skills of doing ministry effectively is not a luxury these days; it's not even an option. More than a few observers of the Church have identified the poor quality of pastoral leadership in our Church as a major problem. All that a newly ordained priest needs today cannot be supplied during seminary training alone.

After the initial formation of the seminary and a period of youthful enthusiasm, there comes a time to take charge of minding your call, a time to stoke the fires of passion and commitment, a time to develop the precise skills needed in priestly ministry, especially the ministry of pastor. Each priest, in the words of II Timothy 1:6, has a duty to take care of "the gift God gave him when hands were laid on him" and to keep that gift "fanned into flame." Pope John Paul II calls it "keeping up one's youthfulness of spirit."

## FORMATION OF PRESBYTERATES

The American Bishops, in *The Basic Plan for the Ongoing Formation of Priests*,[24] note that ongoing formation has two components: the ongoing formation that affects priests individually and the ongoing formation of priests as presbyterates.

The Code of Canon Law[25] says that "seminary students are to be so formed that they are prepared for fraternal union with the diocesan presbyterate." *Intentional Presbyterates: Claiming Our Common Sense of Purpose*, written by this author, was put together for seminarians to help them begin to think about becoming conscious and contributing members of their presbyterates. It was written to fill a vacuum. Even though Canon Law specifically says that seminarians are to be formed for membership in their presbyterates, I could find no seminary that seriously addresses the subject of intentionally integrating new priests into their presbyterates. In most cases, they are left to find their own way.

*The Basic Plan for the Ongoing Formation of Priests* [26] notes that "priests are not priests, one by one, but serve as priests in a presbyterate with their bishop, in what the Catechism calls "an intimate sacramental brotherhood." It also acknowledges that presbyteral formation opens new territory when it says "this corporate sense of priestly identity and mission, although not fully developed even in official documents, is clearly emerging as an important direction for the future." In response to that insight, the new **Institute for Priests and Presbyterates** will offer printed material and practical suggestions to seminarians to help prepare them for "fraternal union with diocesan presbyterates" before ordination, as well as offer some support for presbyteral strengthening after ordination.

Because the priests we have cannot work much harder, in the future they will have to work smarter. They will need, more than ever, to attend to personal growth *and* group unity. Times have changed. It is time for priests to wake up and deal assertively with these new realities. As Francis Bacon put it, "He that will not apply new remedies must expect new evils."

## DISCUSSION STARTERS

1.  Are you concerned about being prepared to handle what a priest is called to handle? In what areas of ministry do you feel you need further formation?

2.  How can you handle your own feelings of having had enough and your need for ongoing formation?

3.  What can you do now, as a seminarian, to prepare yourself for ongoing formation?

4.  What information would you have liked to have about your presbyterate before ordination? What could your diocese do to better bring you in to your presbyterate?

5.  In what special area of ministry would you like more training? Is that training available to you? How will your diocese support you in getting that training? What can you do, on your own, to get that training if your diocese cannot support you?

# CONCLUSION

*Deliver us, Lord, from every evil and grant us peace in our day.*
*Keep us free from sin and protect us from all anxiety as we wait*
*in joyful hope for the coming of our Savior, Jesus Christ.*
From the Mass

Knowing what to do when the honeymoon is over is essential in priesthood as well as in marriage. There will come a time, after finally making it through the seminary, when the adulation of the ordination and Mass of Thanksgiving will stop and the routine and difficult work of parish ministry will set in. Even though it is perfectly normal, for many it is a time of crisis. In marriage, it happens around the seventh year. In priesthood, it happens often within, but is not restricted to, the first five years.

Whether it comes early or late, I believe every priest ought to expect it and prepare himself for it. With 10% to 15% of newly ordained priests leaving in their first five years, it is something that needs to be faced and planned for. It's not a matter of if, but when. Remember, there is no need to panic. It is normal.

Jeremiah, a man called at a very early age, is a model of fidelity in spite of crushing disappointment in ministry. Jeremiah 20:7 has many weak translations. Some translate the Hebrew with dupe: "You duped me and I let myself be duped." (NAB) Or, "You deceived me and I was deceived." (RSV) Rabbi Abraham Heschel, who translates the verse freely and accurately, expresses the thought: "With you, God, I experienced the sweetness of seduction and the violence of rape." To paraphrase a famous country music song, it is after this that Jeremiah gives his "Take this job and shove it, I ain't workin' here no more" speech, only to conclude, like Peter did when so many walked away from Jesus, "Where else can I go?"

Most priests do not experience the acute and piercing disappointment of Jeremiah, but rather a periodic, if not chronic, low-grade version of "I never thought it would be like this." This is when priests are most vulnerable. This is when the grass looks greener on the other side of the fence, when they harbor thoughts of what it would be like to leave. Today, 10% to 15% of the newly ordained act on those feelings.

Even though loneliness is cited as the main reason for leaving, loneliness may be a *result* of the real problem of not being prepared for the reality of priestly life versus the idealization of priesthood in the seminary. Loneliness may be closely connected to feelings of disappointment at having to revise their expectations for ministry and the work involved in doing it and/or feelings of being overextended, unprepared and fundamentally alone.

Timothy, fellow missionary of Paul, was a young man who faced his own crisis at the beginning of his ministry and offers us a model of fidelity in spite of crushing disappointment. In his second letter to Timothy, Paul writes to a young man who wants to give up and come home. Paul reminds Timothy that the Spirit gives pastoral ministers three things during times like this to continue our work: *dunymis, agape* and *sophronismos,* or strength, practical help and the ability to control oneself in the face of panic.

Every priest, if he is to survive and thrive in today's Church, must find that peaceful center, that innermost calm that no storm can shake, that anxiety-free place where one waits in joyful hope, that place of grace under pressure, that solid foundation on which his house can withstand any storm, that peace of mind and heart that only God can give. This is why the prayer life of a priest is so essential.

These times of crisis are normal. They are to be expected. They are not signs that we have made a mistake, but signs that we are on the right path. If they are normal and to be expected, then we need to develop the inner strength to face them, deal with them and overcome them. Eleanor Roosevelt put it this way, "You gain strength, courage and confidence every time you look fear in the face. We must do the thing we think we cannot do." Why must we do it? In the end, we must not forget the words of Jesus to us, "It was not you who chose me. It was I who chose you."

I wish all of you *dunymis, agape* and *sophronismos* – strength, practical help and the ability to know what to do in the face of panic. You *can* do this! You *must* do this! The Church *needs* you. "May the Lord bring to completion the good work begun in you." I leave you with a favorite poem by Rudyard Kipling that seems to be appropriate.

# If

If you can keep your head when all about you
Are losing theirs and blaming it on you,
If you can trust yourself when all men doubt you
But make allowance for their doubting too,
If you can wait and not be tired by waiting,
Or being lied about, don't deal in lies,
Or being hated, don't give way to hating,
And yet don't look too good, nor talk too wise:

If you can dream – and not make dreams your master,
If you can think – and not make thoughts your aim;
If you can meet with Triumph and Disaster
And treat those two imposters just the same;
If you can bear to hear the truth you've spoken
Twisted by knaves to make a trap for fools,
Or watch the things you gave your life to, broken,
And stoop and build 'em up with worn-out tools:

If you can make one heap of all your winnings
And risk it all on one turn of pitch-and-toss,
And lose, and start again at your beginnings
And never breathe a word about your loss;
If you can force your heart and nerve and sinew
To serve your turn long after they are gone,

And so hold on when there is nothing in you
Except the Will which says to them; "Hold on!"

If you can talk with crowds and keep your virtue,
Or walk with kings–nor lose the common touch,
If neither foes nor loving friends can hurt you;
If all men count with you, but none too much,
If you can fill the unforgiving minute
With sixty seconds' worth of distance run,
Yours is the earth and everything that's in it,
And – which is more – you'll be a Man, my son!

What I want you to know is this: You have a choice to make. Will you leave your happiness and effectiveness as a priest to chance, or will you take charge of building it for yourself, from within? Failing to act is to choose. A favorite quote from George Bernard Shaw also seems to be appropriate here.

*This is the true joy in life, the being used for a purpose recognized by yourself as a mighty one; the being thoroughly worn out before you are thrown on the scrap heap; the being a force of nature instead of a feverish selfish little clod of ailments and grievances complaining that the world will not devote itself to making you happy.*

Finally, let me share another of my favorite quotes by W.H. Murray. It serves as a reminder that the God who called us to this work stands ready to help, empower and equip us for ministry. We are not in this alone. Once we commit, help is on its way.

*Until one is committed, there is hesitancy, the chance to draw back, always ineffectiveness. Concerning all acts of initiative (and creation) there is one elementary truth, the ignorance of which kills countless ideas and splendid plans: that the moment one definitely commits oneself, then Providence moves too. All sorts of things occur to help one that would never otherwise have occurred. A whole stream of events issues from the decision, raising in one's favor all manner of unforeseen incidents and meetings and material assistance, which no man could have dreamed would have come his way.*

The secret to unleashing all this help, and the bottom line of this book, is *deep commitment*. Everything depends on how seriously we are committed, not just to *being* a priest, but to *priesting*.

---

## DISCUSSION STARTERS

1. Like St. Peter on the mountain of transfiguration, you cannot stay on top of the world forever. The honeymoon following ordination does not last. The grass will look greener on the other side of the fence. Do you understand that this is a normal part of every calling?

2. What coping mechanisms have you developed to weather such times in your priesthood?

3. What strategies can you envision for yourself that could prevent these episodes from happening too often?

4. How can people help you when you are overwhelmed and overcome by circumstances beyond your control?

5. Is there anyone you admire for having survived painful disappointment? What can you learn from them?

---

# END NOTES

[1] The Basic Plan for the Ongoing Formation of Priests. United States Catholic Conference, Inc., Washington, DC, 2001, Part Two.

[2] Pope John Paul II, I Will Give You Shepherds. St. Paul Books & Media, Boston, MA, 1992, no. 76.

[3] L'Osservatore Romano, 42. Vatican City, October 15, 1990, p. 3.

[4] Philibert, Paul J., O.P., Stewards of God's Mysteries. The Liturgical Press, Collegeville, MN, April 2004, pp. 58-60.

[5] The Priest and the Third Christian Millennium: Teacher of the Word, Minister of the Sacraments, and Leader of the Community. Vatican City, Congregation for the Clergy, 1999, p. 35.

[6] Ibid., p. 40.

[7] Bausch, William J., *Take Heart, Father*. Twenty-Third Publications, Mystic, CT, September 1986.

[8] Walsh, Eugene A., S.S., *Talking With Adults: Practical Suggestions for Preaching, Teaching, Evangelizing*. Pastoral Arts Associates of North America, 1980.

[9] Zander, Rosamund Stone and Benjamin Zander, *The Art of Possibility: Transforming Professional and Personal Life*. Harvard Business School Press, Boston, MA, 2000, p. 108.

[10] Abbott, Walter M., General Editor, and Joseph Gallagher, Translation Editor, "Pope John's Opening Speech," *Documents of Vatican II*, New York, NY, 1966, pp. 715-716.

[11] Talitman, Erin, Ph.D., and Philip Dodson, in *Covenant*, Vol. 19, no. 2, September 2004. Southdown Institute, Aurora, Ontario, Canada.

[12] Cozzens, Donald B., in *Being a Priest*, "The Spirituality of the Diocesan Priest." The Liturgical Press, Collegeville, MN, 1992.

[13] Abbott, Walter M., General Editor, and Joseph Gallagher, Translation Editor, "Decree on the Ministry and Life of Priests," *Documents of Vatican II*, New York, NY, 1966, Chapter II.

[14] Ibid.

[15] Ibid.

[16] Abbott, Walter M., General Editor, and Joseph Gallagher, Translation Editor, "Dogmatic Constitution on Divine Revelation," *Documents of Vatican II*, New York, NY, 1966, Chapter 6, no. 21.

[17] Abbott, Walter M., General Editor, and Joseph Gallagher, Translation Editor, "Pastoral Constitution on the Church in the Modern World" (Gaudium et Spes), *Documents of Vatican II*, New York, NY, 1966, Chapter 2, no. 62.

[18] *As One Who Serves*. United States Catholic Conference, Washington, DC, 1977.

[19] Decree on the Ministry and Life of Priests, no. 9.

[20] Pope John Paul II, *I Will Give You Shepherds*, no. 76.

[21] Peck, M. Scott, M.D., *The Road Less Traveled*, Simon & Schuster, Inc., New York, NY, 1978.

[22] *I Will Give You Shepherds*, no. 71.

[23] Ibid., no. 79.

[24] *The Basic Plan for the Ongoing Formation of Priests*, p. 93.

[25] *Code of Canon Law*, Canon Law Society of America, Washington, DC, 1983, Canon 245, no. 2.

[26] *The Basic Plan for the Ongoing Formation of Priests*, p. 93.

# BIBLIOGRAPHY

Abbott, Walter M., General Editor, and Joseph Gallagher, Translation Editor, "Decree on the Ministry and Life of Priests," *Documents of Vatican II*, New York, NY, 1966.

Abbott, Walter M., General Editor, and Joseph Gallagher, Translation Editor, "Dogmatic Constitution on Divine Revelation," *Documents of Vatican II*, New York, NY, 1966.

Abbott, Walter M., General Editor, and Joseph Gallagher, Translation Editor, "Pastoral Constitution on the Church in the Modern World" *(Gaudium et Spes)*, *Documents of Vatican II*, New York, NY, 1966.

Abbott, Walter M., General Editor, and Joseph Gallagher, Translation Editor, "Pope John's Opening Speech," *Documents of Vatican II*, New York, NY, 1966.

*As One Who Serves*. United States Catholic Conference, Washington, DC, 1977.

Bausch, William J., *Take Heart, Father*. Twenty-Third Publications, Mystic, CT, September 1986.

*Code of Canon Law*, Canon Law Society of America, Washington, DC, 1983.

Cozzens, Donald B., in *Being a Priest*, "The Spirituality of the Diocesan Priest." The Liturgical Press, Collegeville, MN, 1992.

*L'Osservatore Romano*, 42. Vatican City, October 15, 1990.

Peck, M. Scott, M.D., *The Road Less Traveled*, Simon & Schuster, Inc., New York, NY, 1978.

Philibert, Paul J., O.P., Stewards of God's Mysteries. The Liturgical Press, Collegeville, MN, April 2004.

Pope John Paul II, I Will Give You Shepherds. St. Paul Books & Media, Boston, MA, 1992.

Talitman, Erin, Ph.D., and Philip Dodson, *Covenant*, Vol. 19, no. 2, September 2004. Southdown Institute, Aurora, Ontario, Canada.

*The Basic Plan for the Ongoing Formation of Priests*. United States Catholic Conference, Inc., Washington, DC, 2001.

*The Priest and the Third Christian Millennium: Teacher of the Word, Minister of the Sacraments, and Leader of the Community.* Vatican City, Congregation for the Clergy, 1999.

Walsh, Eugene A., S.S., *Talking With Adults: Practical Suggestions for Preaching, Teaching, Evangelizing.* Pastoral Arts Associates of North America, 1980.

Zander, Rosamund Stone and Benjamin Zander, *The Art of Possibility: Transforming Professional and Personal Life.* Harvard Business School Press, Boston, MA, 2000.

Made in the USA
Coppell, TX
12 June 2021